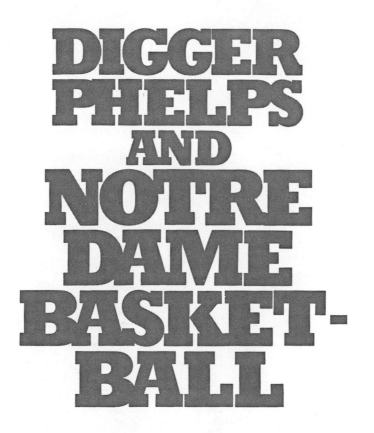

DIGGER PHELPS AND NOTRE DAME BASKETBALL

DIGGER PHELPS AND NOTRE DAME BASKET- BALL

by Richard 'Digger' Phelps & Pat Scanlon

PRENTICE-HALL, INC., Englewood Cliffs, N.J.

Digger Phelps and Notre Dame Basketball
by Richard "Digger" Phelps and Pat Scanlon
Copyright © 1981 by Richard "Digger" Phelps
and Pat Scanlon
Copyright under International and Pan American
Copyright Conventions
Address inquiries to Prentice-Hall, Inc.,
Englewood Cliffs, N.J. 07632
Printed in the United States of America
Prentice-Hall International, Inc., London
Prentice-Hall of Australia, Pty. Ltd., Sydney
Prentice-Hall of Canada, Ltd., Toronto
Prentice-Hall of India Private Ltd., New Delhi
Prentice-Hall of Japan, Inc., Tokyo
Prentice-Hall of Southeast Asia Pte. Ltd., Singapore
Whitehall Books Limited, Wellington, New Zealand

10 9 8 7 6 5 4 3 2 1

Library of Congress Cataloging in Publication Data

Phelps, Richard.
Digger Phelps and Notre Dame basketball.
1. Phelps, Richard. 2. Basketball coaches—
United States—Biography. 3. Notre Dame,
Ind. University—Basketball. 4. Basketball coaching.
I. Scanlon, Pat, joint author. II. Title.
GV884.P45A34   796.32'3'0924 [B]   81-43
ISBN 0-13-211888-2

To my wife, Terry,
and our children Karen, Rick, and Jennifer

Digger

To my parents for the opportunity,
and to my wife and main supporter, Jamye

Pat Scanlon

Our thanks to the Notre Dame Sports Information Department, Roger Valdiserri, John Heisler, and Karen Croake. Also to photographers Brother Charles McBride, F. Edward Ballots, Brian M. Watkins, and Tom Jackman with an assist to Paul Mullaney.

Contents

Introduction

For seven months I found myself living a journalist and basketball fan's dream, watching the drama of a college basketball season unfold, with "inside" knowledge of each coaching move, strategic change, and motivational plan. From the scouting reports, to the development of the game plan, to the practices of implementing the strategy to the game itself, I could stand on the sidelines like an invisible observer, absorbing every move, every bit of information and dialogue. On game days I sat in the Irish locker room and watched Digger Phelps instruct players for the challenge to come, charting the strategy on the board with his left-handed scrawl, standing before his players like a classroom instructor exhorting his students to heed his lecture. When the players trotted out to warm up, I could stay behind to sample Digger's opinion, but often I found myself telling him the details of a story I might be covering for my station, or other non-basketball events. Even moments before a game Digger was interested in more than the event at hand; he didn't let much escape him. Then, on schedule, as the players returned to the locker room, it would be back to basketball and that night's game. There would be more instruction, some inspirational words, the best last—something to really pump up the team, as Digger would say. Digger could be a picture of patience or a man possessed, whichever the situation called for. But as the team exited for introductions, a wink or a grin would sometimes give away the coach's inner thoughts. Yet he could never let the team gain that knowledge.

As the game began I would take my seat in the press box, armed with that special inside information and, unfortunately, a sense of honor that wouldn't allow me to divulge an iota of what had transpired. It was like knowing the identity of Superman, but being sworn to secrecy.

Sometimes it meant biting my lip while others interpreted a coaching move, offering their personal criticisms of a game situation without knowing what the objective was or how successful it might be if executed correctly. From the time I entered the arena until two or three hours later, when I would sit down in front of my typewriter to record it, the frustration of knowing so much but saying so little would burn inside. Still, being a part of the Irish program and getting such a candid look at Digger and his coaching far out-weighed the burden of that bottled-up knowledge.

In fact, it was a position to be envied, one that few others would ever experience and enjoy. There were other side effects of my insider's role that resulted from being in on whatever meeting. Through numerous trips with Digger I learned of the grueling schedule a college coach must keep during the season amidst games, recruiting trips, and speaking engagements. Privacy is precious and one can easily understand why Digger plans his escapes from basketball, for himself and his players, throughout the season.

At times while traveling with Digger I also felt indignation when a fan or sportscaster might second-guess a bit of coaching style or adjustment. When the Irish performed as expected, knock-ing off De Paul or beating UCLA twice, it was evident all the world loves a winner. But following a defeat or lackluster performance, the atmosphere changed dramatically and there were few accolades for a valiant effort. The spirit of the amateur game was often lost with the final score, and the coaches and players were left with the chore of regrouping. Sometimes the game plan deserved better execution; sometimes the players deserved a better fate.

Through it all I realized the complexity of Digger's person-ality as I heard the latest scuttlebutt about his quirks and his alleged egomania and weighed each rumor for its veracity. It is true that he is a demanding coach, but the demands he places on his players and assistants are in fact no greater than those he places on himself. At times it was clear why he had to be harsh and protective of his own time for family and friends: the basketball schedule has its own way of eating into the hours of every day.

Digger's personality struck me as similar to that portrayed by George C. Scott in *Patton*. The burning desire to win, the demand for a full commitment, and the idiosyncrasies—all are marks of a

superior mind. The obsession with gold rings and chains evokes the
pearl-handled revolvers that hung from Patton's hips. At times, while
Digger led his team about the country to different battle sites, it was
easy to envision the movie scene of Patton instructing his officers on
the historical background of those areas; not so oddly, fascination
with history is a trait common to both men. And, in retrospect, I can
think of countless other similarities.

In writing the story of a season's basketball with Phelps, I see
sports as a string of special moments, and although this book is not
a fairy tale about winning championships it is the true account of a
basketball season where a college team did *not* win the national
championship. I hope the narrative illuminates the college basketball game—and one of its top coaches and educators.

Even Patton didn't always win.

Foreword

Having completed fourteen years of college coaching, including nine years at the University of Notre Dame, I have developed some insights into college athletics (basketball), academics, and attitudes, which I call the Three A's.

It is obvious that basketball has grown both positively and negatively over the last decade. Not just in appeal for the action on the court, but also in terms of the high school and college programs that surround the game.

In college, I find that academics are the most misleading of the three A's, owing to weaker admission requirements for most national college programs. I would like to see a survey conducted to determine how many student athletes graduate and what types of degrees they are acquiring. The deterioration of education in college is not unlike the general weakening of education for the mass population over the last decade.

In this book I frequently refer to the NCAA, of which Notre Dame is a member. The major misconception about the National Collegiate Athletic Association is that it is composed of a small group of administrators in Shawnee Mission, Kansas. Every school belongs to the NCAA and the organization is nothing more than whatever the member schools make it. As a member institution Notre Dame receives one vote on all legislation and the majority vote passes or rejects any new rulings. Notre Dame may not always agree with the vote, but we must comply with all legislation (such as the freshman eligibility policy).

If there are infractions of our NCAA legislation, then the investigating force from the national office gets involved. The most difficult situation for the investigators is documenting infractions with solid proof, since most violations involve cash transactions between indirect friends or alumni of a university. Some frequent violations stem from providing athletes cash for spending, game tickets, cars, apartments, or clothes. Like any organization, the NCAA has a disciplinary committee, and member institutions must live with its decisions. We are all under one roof and "they" or "the NCAA" is actually all of us.

Through my experiences with the academics and athletics I arrive at the essential ingredient, attitude. In my estimation, this is the most important element of development an athlete goes through in college. Unfortunately, with the weakening of educational requirements for matriculation and the growing emphasis on winning national championships, the college athlete's attitude may also be a "victim" of the system. The willingness to allow student-athletes to transfer from one school to another; campus violations; recruiting violations; and ego trips for the athlete and his family—and even his coach—all affect his attitude, adversely.

In reading this book you may get the impression that I am demanding or overly critical of the players. In educating these young men on and off the basketball court, I'm trying to prepare them for survival in the world they'll face after their four years at Notre Dame. The situations that I write of—on the basketball court, in the locker room, or in the classroom—are frank descriptions of important events in the team's development as players and as people. This letter from a corporate vice-president prior to a conference I addressed may give you some insight into my coaching personality as a basketball coach and educator.

Dear "Digger":

As our Presidents' meeting draws nearer, I thought I would send you some additional background information on the company and the meeting.

Accordingly, I am attaching a rough draft of the agenda for the meeting. Hopefully, this material will give you a feel for the company as it officially perceives itself.

Insofar as our conference theme of "Winning" is concerned, it is apparent that the company has problems which do not show up in the printed material—other than the eroding financial performance shown in the annual report.

The problems as we see them are:

- A growing bureaucracy which seems more and more remote from the real world of operations. It feels like the staff exists for itself and its various audiences such as the government and has forgotten that its primary purpose is to help the operating people.
- This inward turning has left the bureaucracy feeling that what they do doesn't matter to the business. They rarely think—Where can I save money for the company? —Where can I make money for the company?
- Similarly several of our operating people believe their job is to—
  - Install a manufacturing materials control system; *not* improve profits x dollars by installing a materials control system

    or,
  - gain market share from a competitor; *not* what are the benefits of gaining market share and what are the costs required to do it.

    or
  - protect the operations for the future by not cutting back on employee levels even though some of our businesses are in a deep recession.

Actually, we believe that all organizations experience these problems to some degree or another, but we are convinced that the difference between winning and losing is the attitude and talent that any group brings to the game. We believe we have the talent, what we think is lacking is the attitude and the self-discipline required to turn sporadic performance into consistently excellent performance.

Our team goals and shortcomings are not unlike the atmosphere of the business world, and in many ways a basketball season cannot be measured by winning and losing games; it must also be judged in the manner by which the wins and losses are achieved.

In this book we'll be looking at the three A's, and I'll try to share with you the reality of what's happening. I hope the diagrams, the season, the personalities, the recruiting, the strategies, and the adjustments will give you one coach's honest view of life in athletics.

PART ONE
THE
COACH

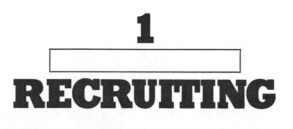

1

RECRUITING

One good night on a recruiting trip can earn a school an NCAA bid two years down the road.

That, simply, sums up recruiting. It is that thought that keeps Digger Phelps and his assistant coaches on the recruiting trail. Persuading high school seniors to attend Notre Dame and play basketball is the foundation of the basketball program. The final success depends on the strength of the foundation. A weak foundation can cause a program to come crumbling down. Good recruiting is the difference between reaching the Final Four of the NCAA tourney and missing the tournament altogether. Once a basketball program reaches a plateau of success, it is strong recruiting year after year that helps maintain the school's position. Digger certainly appreciates the importance of getting the right high school players to attend Notre Dame. Seven straight NCAA Tournament appearances is a record no other college coach has been able to match.

But a coach has to set priorities and goals for recruiting. He has to determine the type of player he needs years ahead. That means recruiting a player to fill a vacancy that will develop in two or three years. Or it might involve strengthening a position where a team is weak or shallow. Often a coach will go after a high school ball handler when his varsity guard is a junior. Then the coach has the time to introduce the incoming freshman to his system of playing, and ease him into the pressures of college life on and off the court. Digger feels strongly about preparing his freshmen for what's ahead. College life is a drastic change from living at home. Additionally, it means competing academically against excellent students and playing basketball against the best athletes in the country. If a player isn't indoctrinated into college life properly, he can lose confidence and become a class or team casualty. Digger and his assistants keep a close watch on how their freshmen are doing in the classroom—and in the dormitory, too. Players sometimes get into trouble academically. As a freshman Bill Laimbeer didn't apply himself in class, became ineligible after his first semester, and flunked out after his second semester; he wound up attending a junior college in Toledo in his sophomore year before earning enough grade points to return to Notre Dame. Digger works hard to destroy any preconception that basketball players at Notre Dame will receive passing grades because of their performance on the court. Unfortunately, some players have to find out for themselves. Academic casualties are a factor that cannot always be anticipated when recruiting. It's one of the elements coaches try to detect when selecting the player to pursue for their program.

Once a coach knows the type of player or position he needs, the recruiting program begins to get very selective. In some years the skills or attitude a coach is looking for do not seem to be available in the nation's senior classes. Or the best high school seniors may not qualify academically. And, of course, there's always the possibility that a school might not fit the requirements of the student player.

"At Notre Dame, we usually start out looking at fifty kids who might fit what we're looking for," says Digger. "Out of that number, maybe half could get into school academically. After you weed out the players who have agents and are talking more than a one-year scholarship, we're looking at a field of twelve."

Unfortunately, the common recruiting practices of some schools differ very much from the NCAA rules. Says Digger: "Cheating is widespread in college recruiting. The NCAA does a pretty good job of policing the obvious violations, but sometimes the violations aren't direct. Maybe something is done unofficially by an overzealous alumnus. But it goes on." And there are still attempts to steal players, even after they have started classes. According to Danny Nee, the Irish recruiting coordinator, "We run into some unscrupulous vultures who call our players and tell them they can transfer, get more playing time, or whatever. Some of the phone calls the players get are absolutely amazing."

When the field of possible recruits is narrowed, the coaching staff attempts to rank the players available. Estimates of which players will blend with the team and complement the present squad are considered. Sometimes speed or shooting ability has to be sacrificed to some degree to recruit a player who will contribute to the team concept. "After the recruiting season is over, newspapers and magazines rate which colleges had the best recruiting years," says Nee. "They are frequently wrong. I think the best recruiting years we've had at Notre Dame have been when we've gone out and signed the players that fit in with the team and play whatever role Digger asks." Digger would love to have ten of the nation's best shooters, ball handlers, and rebounders. But the fact remains that there's only one basketball, and only one player can shoot it at a time. Sometimes successful recruiting means bringing in a few outstanding athletes and matching the rest of the team to complement their abilities. When the Irish team played its way into the Final Four at St. Louis in 1978, the leading scorer on the team was Dave Batton, who averaged fourteen points a game. But between Duck Williams, Kelly Tripucka, and Batton the team clicked. Overrecruiting can be as dangerous as half-hearted attempts.

"It's like a puzzle," Digger remarks. "You have to go out and put the pieces together through a good recruiting program." Also, it is a "now" situation. If a player is available and he's what your program needs, go after him. High school talent is like the stock market; sometimes there are good investments available, a year later there might not be. But if you are successful and get the players you need for the next two or three years, don't go out and overrecruit the following year. "When Gil Salinas and Orlando Woolridge were freshmen, we knew they had the potential to be strong, front-line players for three years. We decided and told them we weren't going to look at any other forwards, just a guard to replace Jeff Carpenter and Duck Williams. He turned out to be Mike Mitchell."

Making the commitment to those two players did two things. It motivated them to work hard in the off season to improve their games. It also headed off any discontent that could occur if Digger brought in a couple of new forwards who might have to sit on the bench. "It's only natural, everyone thinks they should be playing," admits Phelps. "By not red-shirting players or bringing in junior college players, we feel we can get more out of our players by showing we believe in them and by living with them for four years. It helps you recruit a high school senior because he knows you won't grab that J.C. transfer, you'll stick with him."

Phelps has never become concerned with the number of scholarships he still has available. As long as he has eight or nine quality ball players on the team in a year, he's satisfied. During the 1976–77 season, he had his nucleus and blended in walk-ons to fill out the roster. His "S.W.A.T. Squad," walk-ons Chris Fabian, Tim Healy, and Bill Sahm, teamed with scholarship athletes Randy Haefner and Jeff Carpenter. It was a role Phelps created for the group. The fivesome would enter the game in the last few minutes if the Irish were ahead. The band played the S.W.A.T. TV show theme song as they came on. The five received recognition and playing time and they were happy with their role.

"At Notre Dame, you can get top-quality athletes as long as you don't have too many of them," notes Digger. "If you start messing around with more than thirteen, you're fooling with kids who will be unhappy and maybe even transfer. That can lead to problems on the team and work as a tool for other coaches to recruit against you."

Knowing the type of player you want and getting him to enroll in your school are two different matters. Picking the high school seniors you need is the easy task; it's the competition of coach against coach and institution against institution that determines the winning recruiter in the long run. The right approach has to be calculated. Do you come on strong with a sales pitch selling your school and team, or do you take the low-key style, telling the player your thoughts and letting the decision lie in his hands without any interference?

It would seem that the Irish coaching staff shouldn't have much difficulty recruiting. The winning tradition at Notre Dame, the glamour of national television coverage, the excellent academic opportunity and beautiful campus should be enough to win over any recruit. It doesn't work that way, though.

"You have to be a salesman as a head coach now," explains Danny Nee. "It used to be that assistant coaches would handle the recruiting and then a head coach would become involved after the college season was over. Now it's gotten to the point where you scout kids between their junior and senior years in high school at summer basketball camps. If you don't, a kid feels slighted because another school was there to look at him and Notre Dame wasn't."

Over the last five years Digger has emerged as one of the strongest recruiters in the nation. This may be partly because he is a born salesman; he can communicate the positive points of the university in terms a high school student can understand. More important, Phelps conveys an honest picture of college life. There's no reason why he should lie. If he is interested in a player, he'll make a commitment to him. Once he has a man signed, he will call the other candidates and explain the situation, advising them to begin concentrating on some of the other interested schools.

"What I explain to a player," he says, "is that at Notre Dame he can have the opportunity to get a great education, become a part of an institution that will help him for the rest of his life, and still play for a college basketball power. If a kid is looking for the perfect school, he's not attacking the situation properly. There is no perfect school, and if that's what he wants he'll never be happy at Notre Dame or anywhere else. You have to look at the total experience, not just athletics or academics. If you evaluate the situation properly at first, there's no need to transfer, and you live through it." Many people, including the NCAA, allow room for poor judgment and mistakes by condoning transfers from school to school. Digger doesn't: "There are other things that you learn to adjust to in life and the sooner you learn to bear with a situation and not run away, I think it will make you a better all-round person."

Sometimes Notre Dame's basketball program appears more attractive after a recruit has selected a college and he is enrolled. Jeff Rulland, a New York player whom Phelps wanted badly, decided to attend Iona College. But before a Marquette game during his sophomore year, he called, asking to transfer to Notre Dame. Without being vindictive, Digger advised Rulland to stick it out at Iona because he'd be a better person for it.

The same held true for UCLA's Brad Holland and Roy Hamilton. During his freshman year, Hamilton was unhappy with the way things were going. He and David Greenwood, both of Verbum Dei High School, had been recruited by the Irish staff but chose UCLA instead. "I told Father James, a priest at their high school and a great friend of ours, to tell Roy to stay with UCLA," Phelps recalls. "Brad Holland was the same. I hate to see kids transfer." Nee concurs: "The NCAA is taking the allegiance to one's school out of college basketball and serving the athlete's ego. They're not thinking of the kids when they make it easy to hop from school to school." Comparing transferring schools to life, Digger points out that you can't change jobs every day: "We all need our tails kicked at one time or another. Whether it's playing or coaching, socially or professionally, there have to be some tough days to make you a better person. Transferring may be another sign of the times—that we're getting soft as a people."

It's that attitude that characterizes Digger's recruiting style. Sometimes he'll play a low-key role, staying in the background after he knows he's made his philosophy and feelings clear to the player; he'll see to it that his assistants watch a few of the player's games during the year and stay in touch. Other times, when he is competing with a high-pressure coach, he has to become more active. Usually, that means attending a recruit's game whenever Notre Dame's schedule permits, making sure the kid knows Digger is as interested in him as any other coach. And when Digger does show up at a high school game, he makes sure the situation is right. He will say hello to the parents, coaches, friends, and the recruit himself, to attempt to gain that player's confidence. If he doesn't, another coach will. Although it seems like an effort that marks the high school senior as a prize to be captured, that's the unfortunate progression that college recruiting sometimes follows. For Phelps, the realization that what he is offering is a superior product helps justify the chase. Even then, Notre Dame does not get every recruit it wants; "You lose your share, too," admits Digger.

What made him recognize the hard side of recruiting, he says, was what happened while he was scouting Scott McKanlish, a six-foot-ten-inch forward from Poughkeepsie, New York. Digger was an assistant at Penn at the time, and he felt he had the kid sewed up for Penn. Scott played at Arlington High School, not too far from Beacon, New York, Digger's home town, and that buoyed the recruiter's confidence. One night, though, Scott called Phelps and told him he had decided to go to Virginia—bursting Digger's bubble. "It was like boom, down for the ten count and I couldn't get up. That's when you get christened, when they call and tell you 'you lose'—they are going someplace else. Sometimes, recruiting seems easy when you get a kid; then you get cocky. It's when you lose the battle that it hits you."

2

THE ASSISTANT COACHES

Digger's assistants play a key role in his coaching system. Without the two full-time assistants and a third part-time staff member, the Irish could not have attained the levels of success for which Phelps's teams have been noted over the years.

The three assistants have their own areas of responsibility and authority. Phelps delegates responsibility in generous spoonfuls—in recruiting, scouting, and practice sessions. It's understood that Digger has the final authority in policy matters, administration, and game-related decisions. But he will have no part of yes-men or coaches who go along with his plan when they sense the theory might be off base. Digger demands input. If it's a good idea he'll accept it—although if it's not well thought through, he may explode in anger. That's a part of Digger's personality and a fact that perhaps should be included in the personnel job description for Notre Dame assistant basketball coaches.

"Assistants can't be puppets of a head coach," Phelps emphasizes. "They're paid to make positive contributions to the team through knowledge of the game, and if they don't speak up or offer an idea in a coaching session, how can I know if I'm making a mistake?" Digger realizes that no coach can be infallible and that there are times when he's not reading the situation correctly. An assistant coach must speak up, and if his suggestion is sound, Digger is not beyond changing his mind. "I want my players to know that I think enough of the assistants to trust them in some situations, and that they should listen to those assistants and understand that they are also teachers," he says. "When I was younger, I tried to control every situation and didn't leave the assistants much leeway. Now I give them authority and responsibility, and expect the players to respect them, too. There were times in the past where I would do all the correcting in practice instead of letting the assistants do it. Then, when something important came up and I tried to make a point, the players would think 'Digger's on my back again.'"

In recent years, Digger's assistants have actively participated in practice or blackboard sessions, talking with players about the finer points of executing a play or running a drill to get the most out of it. That isn't to say that Digger remains silent during a practice— far from it: "If there's an important point I feel must be made and I haven't said much, the player will accept my criticism and not get uptight about it." Sometimes an assistant goes through multiple jeopardy, wondering whether to venture a suggestion that Digger might have rejected four out of five times. But Digger says, "I still want these guys to make their point that fifth time because that might be the time I can see that the idea is really right."

By giving the assistants a chance to recruit, by splitting up game-scouting responsibilities, and by holding daily staff meetings that allow assistants to take part in plotting the game strategy and drawing out practice timetables, Digger feels that one of his undercoaches will be ready to do a solid job within four or five years. Even during time-outs, while the players catch their breath and regain their composure, the coaching triumvirate is huddling by itself, firing ideas at Digger while the fourth coach upstairs points out floor patterns that might not be discernable at courtside. After a brief session, Digger will decide on a course of action and then instruct the team during the time remaining.

There are times during a game when an assistant may tend to overcoach, try to cover more than necessary, and leave the players confused with too much information. When this happens, Digger solves the problem by personally feeding all necessary information to the team. Assistant coaches might find this system disheartening under the emotional stress of a game, but Digger is, after all, the head coach. "All I want to do is tone them down," he says. "If one of my assistant coaches can read a situation, then he's that much closer to becoming a head coach. I know there are times when I can be a S.O.B., but at least I realize it and I'm trying to deal with it."

That facet of Digger's personality requires the utmost patience and humility from an assistant, but in the end the young coach will receive firsthand experience in the workings of one of college basketball's finest programs. It's a tradeoff between a little duress and a lot of experience.

Digger's assistant coaches should also draw on coaching experience of their own, be it from high school, junior high, or even summer camps. After coaching at a New Jersey junior high school, at St. Gabriel's High School in Hazelton, Pennsylvania, at the University of Pennsylvania as an assistant, and then graduating to head coaching roles at Fordham and Notre Dame, Phelps wants his own assistants groomed in some sort of coaching style. "If I'm going to accept a recommendation I want to know where the assistant is coming from," he says. "As I worked my way up through the ranks I realized I was developing a philosophy of my own. You have to taste defeat when you make wrong decisions before you really become initiated into the coaching process." Digger also encourages his assistants to coach during the summers in camps whenever possible, regardless of their status as Notre Dame assistant coaches. "Until you develop a philosophy, I don't care how good a recruiter you are—you won't make it as a college coach," he notes.

There are many successful coaches in college basketball who went through a string of poor seasons before polishing their style to a winning philosophy. "I realize now that you have to give college kids more room for adjusting to a situation than I did once," says Digger. "That's a feeling I didn't realize until the last few years."

References to making it as a college coach are meaningful in Digger's comments. Digger wants to help his assistants grow until they're capable of understanding all the aspects of a college program. At that point he'll help them find the right coaching jobs. He feels the final step in any coach's development is when he has to direct his own staff, recruit his players, and make snap judgments in a game situation. "I'm like Bear Bryant," he often laughs. "I train them and then toss them out of the nest."

Since coming to Notre Dame in 1971–72, Phelps has developed four head coaches: Dick DiBiaso of Stanford, Frank McLaughlin of Harvard, Dick Kuchen of the University of California–Berkeley, and, most recently, Danny Nee of Ohio University. Each is a different person and each goes about coaching in his own manner. As Digger would say, "It's their time now," wishing them the best and hoping they too can develop their programs to national prominence.

MUSIC

When Digger Phelps came to Notre Dame as a twenty-nine-year-old coach, music didn't seem to fit into his scheme. The intensity of the young mentor overshadowed the value of lyrics and melodies in basketball. That's not to say that Digger had no use for popular music; he always enjoyed it as a tool to relax, as background that could be heard above the murmur of a cocktail party. But as Digger matured as a person, music became more a part of his life, and music carried over into his coaching role, too.

As a man responsible for motivating himself, his assistants, and his players, Phelps found music to be a great motivating tool. Whether in the locker room before practice, at team meetings, or even during sacred practice-time on the hardcourt, Phelps feeds his players music that he has selected for its message or tempo, or both. Before practice the tone of the song might be loud, the type of composition that can excite a player and "psych" him for the workout ahead. The same melody might also be used before a game, while the players are just arriving or dressing in the locker room. When Digger prepares his team for a game, he has the second-string and walk-on players run through the other team's offensive and defensive arrangements. All players' talents are geared to the specific situation at hand, and that takes care of the technical side of the upcoming contest. But the emotional and psychological sides can't be overlooked, either. "When a team comes out for a pregame warmup," says Digger, "the bands are playing and people are screaming. You have to create a similar situation in practice for the kids." So when Supertramp, the Eagles, Michael Jackson, or Herb Alpert fills Notre Dame's Athletic and Convocation Center arena during a practice, it happens, says Digger, for two reasons: "First, I think music puts the kids in a state where they can be themselves and relax. Also, players like music and it contributes to a learning atmosphere where you can get things across to them."

Digger also realizes that after a day loaded with classes, assignments, and tests, players aren't always fresh when they show up at the court. Add a practice session that lasts between one and two hours to a student-athlete's daily schedule, and the day becomes grueling. Mental stress can sometimes be more fatiguing than a difficult workout. So the teaching, training, and conditioning of a practice session has to be combined with something appealing to an individual.

"Music is a break in routine," says Digger. "It's a reprieve from a structured practice that can be enjoyed by the players or the coaches. In today's pressure game, you have to be able to escape, mentally. If only for a little while." Sometimes, for Digger, the escape doesn't have to be during practice; it can be back in the office while he is answering mail. The getaway can also happen during a brainstorming session with his assistants. "If a song comes on the radio, something I've heard before or just a melody I like, I will tell my secretary, Dottie, not to bother me for a few minutes while I listen to it." He will then look past the letters on his desk or the X's and the O's on the blackboard. Suddenly, the total picture comes into view and he is envisioning the sweet taste of success, college basketball's Final Four.

"Music almost puts you into a cosmos state," he says. "In the modern game, you can take a song with emotion and transfer that feeling to the players, using it as a tool to direct a player's emotions to the goals you're stressing. By listening to a song and becoming absorbed in its lyrics or tempo, you can fantasize about the situation. Music is a vehicle to a fantasy world; if you can connect the reality of what you're trying to accomplish as a team with the dreamy world of a song, the end result can be a team attitude geared toward your goals."

For Irish teams, sitting and listening to a particular song has become a regular part of their weekly routine, as normal as shooting foul shots at the end of the day. With the team gathered in the locker room, Digger seeks to join the emotion of the music being played to the goals he and the team are trying to achieve. He will talk about the Final Four, what it would be like to cut down the nets after a championship victory. It's a scene that every basketball player in the country dreams of, and Digger gives his players a taste of success as they huddle in the familiar setting of their locker room. Although he realizes that as a coach he is creating an atmosphere of fantasy, he still maintains firm control of the situation. A student of music and personalities, Digger draws the tempo of a song into the reality of a college basketball season.

To have a great basketball season there have to be some occurrences that distinguish it from an average season. "For our team," says Digger, "maybe that special note is a win against Kentucky; the tempo building could be Marquette, DePaul, and Dayton as we close out the regular season. Those are the key notes of our schedule that could add up to a great season. And they're exactly like a lasting song."

Take the song "Long Way Home" by Supertramp—one of the theme songs Phelps chose for his team. Digger the coach almost becomes Digger the songwriter as he stands before his team. "Lonely days and lonely nights," goes the song, and Digger remarks, "We all go through them but you have to go forward and take the long way home." Eventually, there's a break in the lyrics while the piano and background harmonicas carry on. "You've got the message," Digger exhorts. "Now here's your chance to reflect on it. Let it all go, let it hang, be yourself, but think about it."

Digger likens music to basketball practice, referring to players struggling through new plays until they grasp it, just as if they were musicians learning a new work. A song builds like a season, he believes, and if a player can visualize its movements as the situations that develop, he's creating a positive mental attitude that can help carry a team to success. He hopes the Irish will go through the season with victories adding up to create a lasting song, one that will be remembered by sports enthusiasts decades from now as they reminisce about college basketball.

Digger's philosophies are never definable within a narrow context. He sees his role as preparing his players for life beyond the basketball court. Likewise, his use of music goes beyond its conventional purpose.

"Music is infinite," he says. "Through the ages a good work, be it Beethoven or Bach, stands as a well-produced thought. No matter how it's been done in the past, however different the beat, tempo, or instruments involved; it's still a work of music. It lasts, like people, through generations and generations. Music is a part of our lives, a simple means of conveying a message through a melody or lyrics or both. The great works not only give you philosophy; they give you direction. Music is a fantastic tool for communicating ideas, and its value extends to basketball as much as any other part of life."

Incorporating music into practice sessions is typical Digger, but it's far from being his only morale-building device. For years his coaching career has been marked by similar psychological ploys, such as cutting down the nets in practice before beating UCLA and ending John Wooden's eighty-eight–game winning streak. Once, his psyching gifts even extended to football. Before Notre Dame played Southern Cal in 1978, he suggested that football coach Dan Devine dress his squad in green jerseys. The result was an Irish victory that carried the team to a national championship.

Digger has the ability to turn a common occurrence into an inspirational tool; it's the same ability possessed by a movie director. "Games are theatrical productions, too," he says. "What I tell the team is that we've got the theme and we've got the music. If we execute correctly and get a few breaks we'll be there in the Final Four. We've got the music—now let's go get the action to go with it."

PART TWO
THE
SEASON

1

CHARITABLE BEGINNINGS

It had been a while since the Irish appeared before the home crowd on the familiar Athletic and Convocation Center floor. Digger's boys closed their 1978–79 season against East Carolina with an 89–72 win. Since then there had been dog shows, the baton-twirling American Youth on Parade, numerous trailer shows, and even former President Gerald Ford, all appearing beneath the same dome that protects the Notre Dame student athletes from the harsh Indiana winters.

After February 26, 1979, the Irish varsity basketball team had been conspicuously absent from the A.C.C. hardcourt as Digger Phelps's squad became a traveling road show, crossing state borders—and even an ocean, to play in Yugoslavia. The only trip the team missed was to Salt Lake City, Utah, site of the NCAA championship game. Michigan State and a player nicknamed "Magic" cancelled Notre Dame's appearance.

With a new season about to start, it was time to step onto familiar turf again. On Sunday, November 11, the southern dome of the center was filled to near capacity. The spectators had come to see the new 1979–80 Irish basketball team in an intrasquad game. And since proceeds for the debut were going to charity, the large crowd was doubly welcome.

"I blew it last year," Digger admitted, as he surveyed the great number of locals who had turned out to get a glimpse of the squad. The remark wasn't in reference to the previous season, or even to the fateful game against Michigan State in the Midwest Regional. Phelps was thinking instead in terms of scheduling and promotions. The charity game is an annual event that showcases the squad and helps raise money for the Special Olympics and a neighborhood tutoring program. "Last year I scheduled this intrasquad game after the Russian game," he said. "The turnout wasn't as good as it could have been, but this year I think we made up for it."

A crowd of 8,700 admirers turned out to catch a glimpse of last year's favorites and the freshmen who were now as big a part of the program as anyone. The striking differences were the veteran frontliners, Kelly Tripucka and Orlando Woolridge. Kelly sported a new, curly hair style for the upcoming season. And Orlando, tagged the "Tree" for his tall court stature, had filled out over the summer, thanks to some long sessions with the weights. Tree's trunk was thicker and his limbs had a distinct definition about them.

There were also a few fresh faces that had been added to the squad since Bill Laimbeer and Bruce Flowers graduated. Tim Andree, Bill Varner, and John Paxson had donned the Irish green for the first time, and their presence was noticed from the start. In terms of importance, an intrasquad scrimmage ranks slightly higher than a daily practice, but it provides an opportunity to ease the newcomers into the game experience, helps make the first few minutes of the regular season a little easier when the time comes. Notre Dame's first opponent would provide enough anxious moments for the frosh, let alone 11,345 screaming students, staff members, and area residents.

"The scrimmage also serves as a conditioning exercise," said Digger, after the endless movement up and down the court had ended. "I needed it tonight, especially for Gilbert." For the man known affectionately on the squad as the "world's tallest Mexican," it hadn't been a good preseason. Gil Salinas developed athlete's foot, then neglected it until he couldn't walk, let alone run. Before the game, the doctor gave Gilbert the green light to play and that was all Digger had to hear. Salinas played thirty-five minutes, part for experience and part for conditioning. Phelps had feared that he wouldn't be able to utilize Gil's size against the Russians four days away; the coaching staff had enough injuries to contend with before that impending international match-up. Mike Mitchell, a sophomore guard, had injured his knee late in September and required surgery before returning to action. Tim Andree, the tall workhorse from Brother Rice High School in Detroit, was hobbling with tendonitis. Other injuries included assorted twisted ankles and sprains that earned Tracy Jackson, Kelly Tripucka, and John Paxson a few days off from practice. Those were injuries that Digger could tolerate during preseason workouts, but no doubt his view would be different when the Irish started the official season.

The continued absence of Paxson and Mitchell was confirmed when Assistant Sports Information Director John Heisler introduced the starting lineups. Marc Kelly and Kevin Hawkins were introduced as starters for the second-string green squad and before long, a third walk-on, Tim Healy, entered the game as a substitute. The trio's participation indicated the extent of the bumps and bruises that had plagued the squad during the last few weeks. Digger realized he had to avoid these injuries if he was to realize his season's goal of a national championship.

"I needed Paxson tonight," he concluded after the scrimmage. "If he had been able to play I probably wouldn't have used Marc, Tim, or Kevin." Freshman John Paxson, the brother of former Dayton star Jim, was in street clothes with a sprained ankle. There was no doubt he'd make a contribution to the program before the season was over, but Digger wanted to ease him into the intricate offensive and defensive systems. The coach feels the transition to college life is hard enough in the classroom and dormitory without overburdening the freshmen with too much court responsibility at first.

Digger has spoken frequently against freshman eligibility. He formed his opinions as he coached at Penn, an Ivy League school. At that time, a freshman wasn't eligible for varsity competition in the Ivy League. The first-year student was allowed to adjust to life away from home, tough academic requirements, and the rigors of competing against some of the nation's top athletes before varsity competition. "If I had my own way, freshmen wouldn't play," says Digger, although adding, "Unfortunately, if I was the only coach to use that rule, recruiting would become impossible when I had to compete against a school that allowed freshmen to play." As a frosh begins his basketball career at Notre Dame now, Digger and his assistants keep a close eye on the progress he's making on the court and in the classroom. At least for the charity game, Paxson didn't have to worry about progressing. His absence opened the door for tiny Marc Kelly, a five-foot-ten walk-on who took advantage of the starting role.

Marc had been away from the hardcourt longer than most of his teammates, thanks to a run-in with the NCAA. He had received some attention for his movie "exploits" in Gabe Kaplan's *Fastbreak*, and the one-line part cost him a trip to Murfreesboro, Tennessee, where the Irish played the first game of the NCAA Midwestern Regional. The fact that a walk-on basketball player for Notre Dame appeared in a box-office hit turned out to be an angle no sportswriter could pass up. It was a story that color commentators and feature writers thrive on, but unfortunately the publicity Marc received began to interest the NCAA investigators in Shawnee Mission, Kansas.

When the NCAA discovered that an Irish basketball player had received $750 to appear in a film about basketball, the watch-guard body immediately declared Marc Kelly ineligible for college athletics. The wrath of the college's own police organization had been invoked. "What followed" says Digger, "was a terrible public relations move by the NCAA, the kind of decision that continues to hurt its image. Here's a kid who is not on scholarship, has back problems, and whom the NCAA declares ineligible because he appeared in *Fastbreak* as a basketball player. There are baseball players who can go out and make $150,000 a year and still play college basketball if they have any eligibility left. But Marc had to pay the money back to the moviemakers before he could be declared eligible again. I think the decision was bad for the NCAA's image."

But how did Notre Dame wind up with Kelly on the team? Digger admits he's not the type of player who could turn an athletic program around. Sometimes, though, there's more to a program than appears in a box score. Marc and Greg Gorgian were starting guards for California's Crescenta Valley High School in their senior year. Digger was interested in Gorgian then, and invited him to visit the campus for the Southern California football weekend. Kelly, being a friend of Gorgian, arranged his admissions interview for the same weekend, and the backcourt pair made the trip to South Bend together. Marc wanted to attend Notre Dame regardless of his chances to play basketball, and there's no doubt an invitation to be a member of the Irish squad was the last thing he expected.

"He's the kind of kid you want to have around a program," reflects Digger. "Marc is gung-ho Notre Dame, and after he tried out as a walk-on we guaranteed him a spot on our roster." Digger was happy that Marc could play a lot in the intrasquad game, especially after losing his trip to the NCAA regionals last spring. "He used to hang out at Pauley Pavilion when we'd play UCLA. In fact he still has Bernard Rencher's wrist bands and someone's old game socks." There's a special place in the Irish program for Marc and the other walk-ons, Kevin Hawkins and Tim Healy. The group has limited ability, yet they get a chance to play major college basketball. The job isn't always glamorous. For Marc it means imitating opposing players—running the offensive pattern other teams will use against the Irish. This prepares the first string for what they'll see during a game.

"It's a tough transition to go from being a high school star to a member of the bomb squad that only sees action if the game is a rout," says Phelps. "Still, Marc accepts the role well. He realizes there are a lot of opportunities he'll get that other students would love to experience."

A practical psychologist, Digger realizes that the handling of the walk-ons can't jeopardize the team's success: "Without meaning any harm to Marc, if we have to rely on his abilities as a five-foot-ten guard we're in trouble or we're not recruiting the right people."

However, Paxson was still bothered with a sprained ankle, so Marc got a chance to start for the green squad. And during the game, he took advantage of every second of the thirty-two minutes he played. He wound up the night with six points, and brought the crowd to its feet when he stole the ball from All-America Kelly Tripucka. That brought accolades from Digger, who noticed the response of the crowd. "I loved it. He played the role we asked of him, too. We needed Marc out there and he came through. I really think we've got the right people on our team."

That fact was obvious to anyone with an eye for basketball. The pinpoint passing, hustle, and the awesome dunking ability of Orlando Woolridge drew the applause of the early-season crowd. Indiana basketball fans are knowledgeable, and since little of importance was riding on the game, a murmur filled the A.C.C. instead of the usual deafening roar.

"It was a good preparation for the Russians," said Digger, as he looked ahead to a game that's been a fixture on the Irish schedule for the last three years. "I'm pleased about the whole night, including the fact that we raised almost twice as much money for the charity fund than we did last year."

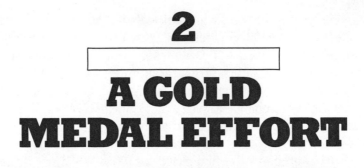

A GOLD
MEDAL EFFORT

Digger Phelps does not take losing lightly. Perhaps that's why two of his assistants, Danny Nee and Tommy McLaughlin, took such a hard look at the Soviet national team. Danny watched them twice against Brigham Young and Colorado, and Tommy's expertise came from observing the Soviets against the University of San Francisco. Notre Dame and the Russians had clashed three times before, once during the Dantley era, in Madison Square Garden, where the Irish lost by one point, 77–76. When the series moved to the A.C.C., Dave Batton and Duck Williams offset a fifteen-point performance by behemoth 7-foot-3 Vladimir Tkachenko, scoring eighteen and fourteen points respectively.

To this day Digger credits a lot of the victory to his frequently used home weapon, the student body. "Alexandr Gomelsky, coach of the Soviet team, chose the wrong end of the court," he says. "In the second half they had to shoot in front of the student body and that drove them crazy." A thirteen-point spurt by the Irish midway through the first half didn't hurt, either.

It was the 1979 loss before the home fans that left Digger smarting as he and his coaches prepared their strategy and game plan for the upcoming contest. Gomelsky had chosen the right basket in 1979, building 13–4 and 25–10 leads in the first twenty minutes. With the Irish stumbling along under the unfamiliar international rules, the veteran Soviet squad never looked back. Utilizing a few new wrinkles, Gomelsky beat Phelps's club, 90–75. That was what really irked Digger.

He acknowledged that the Soviets were better at the transition game, and that the international rules enabled the Russians to leave his club behind, he said. But deep down, Digger knew he and his staff weren't prepared for what was up Gomelsky's sleeve. One might ask how anyone could know the game's impending strategy, but Digger didn't see it that way. He thinks he should always weigh every possibility; and this year, with the Moscow Olympic Games rapidly approaching, his desire to beat an older, more experienced Soviet team was clearly evident.

The coaches' sessions were intense. "We're going to be in one of our offenses, inbounding the ball—and boom, they're going to trap the ball," remarked Danny Nee. "It's just something they do; it's not premeditated or a set play." Danny, then senior assistant coach, wasn't concerned about the Soviets trapping the guards as they brought the ball upcourt. He'd seen the Russians play twice and it was his opinion there was no need to install a special offense. "I'll talk with the guards about it; they'll just have to read it," he said. Digger countered, "Let me throw this at you. We weren't ready last year for them to start picking us up at the foul line. If Alexandr is sitting out there now thinking up another surprise, what kind of surprise can he come up with?" He now sounded out each assistant; each one's opinions and observations were wanted and welcome. Then he took over again: "Alex can't press full court because they're too damn slow, right?" Nee concurred: "The only thing he can do is say, 'Dammit, let's hit them there.' That's the last weakness we haven't covered and I don't want to be standing there game night with my pants down, wondering what the hell we should do." Digger said, "That's all *I'm* asking. What can he do? He caught us unprepared last year. That was last year; it's not going to happen this year. So all I'm saying is, we can take five minutes a day this week. We can say 'Hey fellas, let's go over this possibility.' I don't want to see another Pearl Harbor. Then the players won't look at us and say 'Why the hell didn't we go over that this week!'"

The brain picking wasn't over yet. "It's not going to be the way you're thinking," offered Nee. "It isn't going to be a team oriented set-up, come-up-the-court type of trap. It will be out of a zone trap—and I saw them do that."

Bingo. There were no sirens that went off or light bulbs that turned on. But Digger, in a less abrasive tone now, knew he had hit paydirt. He sprang up to the chalkboard on the wall, diagramming what could happen if Gomelsky went an extra step to a trap-zone defense to cause Irish turnovers. Chalk dust floated from the blackboard, covering a collection of old Notre Dame press guides and other basketball magazines sitting on a coffee table below. Before Digger finished, it looked as if the table had been sprayed white.

"If you're Alex and you want to upset Notre Dame in Indiana," he continued, "what's the last thing you can do? He stuck it to us last year with a defense we weren't ready for. We ended up with twenty-seven turnovers and whatever the final count was. Now I'm saying, What's the last thing he can do with his personnel? That's the last element of surprise I can think of and you've got to have something ready for it. He's never shown a point zone, has he?" McLaughlin and Nee shook their heads. "He could, though—he's a tough one," said Digger. The assistants agreed on that possibility and Digger went on. "Alexandr has never shown a point-zone defense, but then he'd never shown the configuration that surprised us last year, either."

Now Digger got to his main point, diagramming the Russians' best defensive pattern on the blackboard. "What if he waits for us to get to the penetration line?" he asked, turning slashes, circles, and scrawlings into Tkachenko, Mishkin, and Eremin. "I could see him doing that," said Nee and McLaughlin simultaneously, and before they could continue Digger sold his point, inserting a specific offensive pattern into the week's list of plays to be taught and executed in practice.

There were three days of preparation before Digger and his staff could find out how well they had planned. And for Digger there were also the other responsibilities that go with a Notre Dame head coaching position—including various public appearances, and a roast for Al McGuire.

There was also a talk with South Bend's Rotarians. Baz O'Hagen, General Manager of WNDU–TV in South Bend—which hosts Digger's pregame show—introduced the man who needed no introduction to local businessmen. "We're anxious to hear the good news you're going to give us about the basketball team this year, and the turnout today reflects the anticipation for the season," said O'Hagen. The lunchtime gathering at the city's Century Center also heard again about Digger's six consecutive trips to the NCAA Regionals, a record no other active coach could—or still can—claim.

But the introductory remarks weren't all praise; O'Hagen couldn't resist a few quick one-liners. He explained that he had asked Ray Meyer and Al McGuire, two of Digger's close friends, for an evaluation of the guest of honor. O'Hagen then read their replies aloud. DePaul Coach Meyer referred to Digger as a philanthropist, saying Digger had been trying for years to give away $10,000 to the family of the unknown soldier. McGuire, who would be roasted later in the evening, used the opportunity to get some advance revenge. He wrote, "The birth of Digger started the Planned Parenthood movement in America." The former Marquette coach also couldn't pass up the chance to refer to Digger's father the undertaker, writing, "There's more imagination in his father's funerals than in the Notre Dame offense."

Finally, the clowning ended and Digger received his chance to espouse his philosophies and his outlook for the upcoming season. "We just want to win it this year," he said.

Over the previous few years, Digger had made his goals clear, laying out a schedule that every Irish fan could recite—and one of the Rotarians did: "Last year there were three goals you set: make grades by the first of the year, win twenty games, and make the NCAA. What about this year?" "Our goal is to win it," Digger repeated. "We'll get a bid so let's just win this sucker. That's all I want to do anyway; I'm tired of being in a position of just going to the regionals."

Then Digger made some strong statements. He was going for broke. He would not be satisfied simply with an invitation to the NCAA Tournament. He felt the field had been "watered down ... a sign of the times as a nation looks for the easy way out ... Let's let everybody play, not work to get to the playoffs. This is where we're starting to soften." Digger contended that the hard-fought competition that previously resulted in a twenty-five team tournament made college basketball more exciting. That was not to say that a conference tournament, played over a few days, to select a representative was within the definition of what Digger defined as proper competition. "You play a season to get to the tournament," he said, speaking out against alliances like the Atlantic Coast Conference that use a tourney to determine which team represents their group. "You don't play one weekend to get there. A team can play hard and win in December, January, and February; but lose early in their conference tournament. Then, despite the fact that they might be one of the best teams in the country, the kids are forgotten. Those kids worked hard to get to the tournament and now they're staying home. I think it's an injustice that teams can work hard all season, fight for a bid, and lose out because of a tournament upset. Couple the fact that we're watering down the NCAA field and taking out the incentive to play hard all season and I think we're committing a double wrong."

This is the type of forum Digger thrives on; he doesn't like to shy away from controversial subjects. In less than half an hour, he took on the NCAA and conference tournaments, and made it clear his only goal was to win the NCAA championship.

His next questioner was blunt. "Did you recruit any speed this year?" "No," replied Digger. "I wouldn't know what to do with it if we recruited speed." The query referred to the rap on the previous year's squad—that Flowers and Laimbeer were too slow. The sarcasm in Digger's retort reflected a twinge of indignation at the criticism. "As a coach, I would love to have ten speedsters, press all day and run, run, run. Coaches are selfish like that. We try to recruit the best talent available to us, but we can't because of several factors." Digger explained the academic restrictions, and said, "Many of the players we compete against couldn't get into Notre Dame." And he added, "There's also the attitude of the kids. Whether they're the fastest kids in the country or not, I want our players to be thoroughbreds as people." The third factor was the clincher; it brought a big crowd reaction. "The final reason is that we're not going to go out and buy speed. Right now that talent is as hot as the gold market. If you find a 6-foot-8 guy who's fast, he's got an agent and he's dealing in cash. The three freshmen we brought in this year are the type of individuals we want at Notre Dame. I couldn't be happier with them."

Digger breathed easier for the next few questions, talking about the television schedule and rule changes. But the reprieve ended when a man wanted to know what Digger thought about the Pan-American Games. The question was obviously loaded, an attempt to unearth a feud between Digger and Bobby Knight, the Indiana coach who had led the United States team. Indiana hadn't been on the Irish schedule for two seasons, and some felt it was because of a conflict between the two coaches. To the surprise of many, Phelps came to the aid of Knight: "We won the gold medal there with a good team and a good coach." But the questioner still pressed Digger, asking, "Is Bobby in trouble?" This referred to a dispute in which Knight had been involved during the Pan-American Games. Digger didn't waste an instant. "No, he got screwed. The State Department blew it and I'll defend Bobby right down to whatever it takes." Digger explained the incident. "The officials in international basketball are inconsistent and you have to understand their interpretations. Bobby questioned an offensive charge in the first game, trying to point out the rule so that some official wouldn't show the same poor judgment later. At the time, the United States team was leading by thirty-five points and the fact that Knight questioned the official looked more like overkill than an attempt to understand an official's judgment. You have to teach that type of situation, especially when you're coaching an all-star team and you're stressing defense."

Digger warmed up to the subject. "I'd do the same thing," he said. "Some night when you're down by a point, that kind of interpretation of the rule could cost you the game. The fact that the media didn't understand Bobby and the coaching move added to the problem. He's a perfectionist. Then, when the Brazilian girls' team disrupted his practice later in the gymnasium, it became a political football. And that's where the State Department blew it. The situation never should have left the gym, even if Bobby and the policemen were both wrong."

Keeping to the international theme, Digger described his team's recent Yugoslavian tour, and painted a picture of the animosity he and his players experienced. "You better believe that there's a lot of anti-American feeling in the world, no matter how much we help their economies, cooperate, or get involved. It even happens in a United States possession like Puerto Rico. When we toured Communist Yugoslavia for two weeks, we never saw anybody from our embassy. If they'd been there at the gym with Bobby and the U.S. team, the problem never would have left the building. But that's where our great State Department blew it and by the time it finally got involved, it was too late."

The dangers of international competition loomed for Digger within the next thirty-six hours. But unlike the difficulties that Bobby Knight faced, the immediate obstacles confronting Digger were tall, skilled, Soviet players.

There also remained the verbal joust with Al McGuire, scheduled to be roasted later that evening in Milwaukee to benefit the Arthritis Foundation. The "Digger and Al Show" was always one

of the finest productions west of Broadway. McGuire, the witty
eccentric who coached Marquette to a national championship,
always managed some of his best antics in the presence of the
undertaker's son. That night wasn't any different.

"This is tough for all of us to get together and make fun of
each other," noted Al. "There are so many things that have to be right
to carry this off without offending one another." Somehow, the
balance was maintained throughout the night.

The cocktail party at Milwaukee's Pfister Hotel looked like a
gathering of Who's Who in college athletics. Ray Meyer, the elder
statesman from DePaul University, was chatting with Billy Packer, the
color commentator who pairs with Dick Enberg and Al for NBC's
nationally televised college basketball coverage. Then there was
Butch Lee, the former Warrior All-American who earned player-of-
the-year honors as a senior. He was talking to the man who helped
him gain those distinctions, Kevin Byrne, the former Marquette
sports information director. Add one of the funniest morning radio
personalities in the country, Charlie Hanson, along with McGuire's
friends and family, and the room was filled with happy and
distinguished guests. As for the star butt of the evening, it was
difficult not to notice him as he mingled with the crowd in a black
velour suit—described as typical McGuire style.

When Digger entered the reception, it was almost as if
someone flipped a switch and turned him on. The man was in his
element, surrounded by coaches, people close to basketball, and
most of all, friends. After a quick greeting from Al, Billy Packer
approached Digger with a business proposition, a clothing line
called Coach's Choice. All the top coaches would be outfitted with
complimentary wardrobes, said Packer. Digger seemed skeptical. "I
hope it's not like the last investment you had for me," he quipped.
Some time earlier, Packer and broadcaster Dick Enberg had been
about to invest in a small commuter airline based in South Bend. It
looked promising, and because of its connection with South Bend,
the pair decided to tell Digger about it. With feigned interest, Digger
asked Packer, "Do you have any idea how many planes the airline
has in its fleet?" Packer responded, "Yes, of course," and Digger
closed with an item that dropped like a bomb. "Well, check on the
number again, and see if that number includes the plane that's lost
somewhere at the bottom of Lake Michigan." It was no wonder the
clothing line sounded too good to be true.

Later, as the party was getting set to move into the packed ballroom, a Japanese friend of McGuire's approached Digger. "Do you remember me?" he asked. Digger didn't bat an eye, "Yeah, Pearl Harbor, right?" Suddenly McGuire and his friend were laughing hysterically. Al claimed it was the best line Digger had ever come up with. But Al had not yet known what he was in for the rest of the night.

Nothing is sacred when a close bunch of friends gather to roast one of its own. That was a lesson that Al learned at the outset when master of ceremonies Charlie Hanson started his routine. Hanson, a morning radio personality for WISN, unleashed the type of humor that characterized his twenty years of broadcasting in the beer capital of the world. He delivered a string of high-powered one-liners that had the ballroom in an uproar—a tough act for the others to follow. Sensing the need for survival, Digger stole a page from McGuire's play book. "Sit down, will you, we're supposed to be the show," cried Digger, gaining an upper hand in much the same way McGuire would when he was losing control of a game. The people loved it, including Hanson, who quickly ad-libbed, "Call a foul on him, and make sure I get one shot."

But the real target, McGuire, was basted by everyone. His coaching style, personality, his TV commentating, and his New York background provided the roasters with plenty of ammunition. When it came time for Digger to get his shots in, the "Digger and Al Show" resumed.

"I can't believe that eight hundred people turned out at one hundred dollars a plate," said Digger. "Even more amazing, half of the crowd are women. The last time I was with you, Al, you paid one hundred dollars to have one girl come see you." The remark might not have made it on Channel 6, a local television station taping the roast to be aired at a later date, but the Pfister crowd responded with a roar.

The final shot, however, was the guest of honor's. The story that Digger told reminded Al McGuire of a time when he and Phelps were staying together at a hotel with their wives. McGuire recalled the pair was in the cocktail lounge waiting for their wives to get ready for dinner. As Al put it, "A lady of the night ... a hooker ... approached us. It seems that Digger couldn't resist playing along with the woman, asking her how much she charged for her services. When she mentioned a price of one hundred dollars, Digger said he wouldn't pay ten dollars." McGuire then went on to tell of how their wives finally arrived and they walked toward the lobby. "Digger was heading for the car, his arm around his wife, when the hooker appeared again. 'See what you get for ten dollars,' she said." The joke left Digger shaking his head, going along with the joke. Of course, it never happened that way—but neither had the situation Digger had referred to earlier. It was all in good fun, and the reaction of the crowd attested to it.

On the trip back across Lake Michigan, Digger explained his friendship with McGuire. "Coaching is like a closed fraternity," he said. "We enjoy each other off the court no matter what happens on the court," stated Digger. "Al and I could rant and rave for forty minutes, but after the buzzer sounded and the yelling stopped we would go out for a beer."

It was McGuire who taught Digger a few lessons in showmanship. When Digger was in his first year at Fordham, the two coaches' teams played at Madison Square Garden. The game was going along smoothly for the upstart Phelps; his Rams were staying with Marquette, and even went up by two points.

"I was sitting on the bench thinking this is the greatest situation in the world," Digger recalled. "There we were in the Garden, a big crowd on hand, and it was just a great seesaw battle." But that soon came to an end. McGuire jumped up the minute his Warriors went down by two points. Immediately, he lit into one of the referees and received a technical foul for his comments. The next thing I know, Marquette explodes and we lose by twenty points." It was then that Digger learned a lesson in coaching showmanship—how to shift the pressure of the game and crowd from his players to himself. Digger often reminds the players and assistant coaches: "Don't worry about the officials or the crowd, let me handle them." McGuire had taught him how to disrupt a game pattern and control the situation, an essential skill for a top-notch coach.

Since then Digger and Al have both won court battles, but through it all there remains a mutual friendship that keeps the pair charter brothers in the close-knit coaching fraternity.

It had finally arrived on November 15—the first chance to face another basketball team. Scrimmage time was over. The reputed best basketball team in the world, the Soviet National squad, was ready to give Digger's crew a lesson in international competition. This same team would represent Russia in the 1980 Olympics. Its youngest member was nineteen years old and its oldest was thirty-five. The Russians dressed quietly and confidently in the A.C.C. visitors' locker room.

Notre Dame's locker room was filled with music, a rowdy rendition of the CBS Sports Spectacular theme blared on the tape player. Players filed in one by one, getting undressed and then taped by trainer Skip Meyer. Managers swarmed over the court and around the room, making sure that their season debut went well, too. Stacy Russo, the head manager, quietly checked his pregame list.

Amidst all the activity, one figure stood out, freshman Tim Andree. Tim had arrived two hours before tip-off. He was taped, in uniform, and nervously strutting around the tiny room. Tim possessed enough nervous energy to leap tall buildings, let alone seven-foot-three-inch Soviets. He stretched, bounced, paced, and combed his hair a few dozen times. Each time he would glance in the mirror, make a few quick passes through his full bangs, and then toss the comb back in his locker. The upcoming game was certainly a big change from Brother Rice High School, and Tim was going to be more than prepared.

Aside from Tim's jitters, the locker room was calm. While the players went through their warmup drills, Digger sat nonchalantly in the locker room. "This game is just as important as a UCLA game to me," he remarked. He was satisfied that the coaches had prepared the team well; it was the uncontrollable elements of the game that he feared the most. He inwardly psyched himself with a Michael Jackson song as he made ready to stand before the team to inspire them.

"This game tonight is for our gold medal," Digger told a now quiet locker room. The players were assembled in a semicircle. The countdown to the tip-off was under way. Slowly, Digger built the team's confidence, reminding them of the hard work and preparation that preceded the game. He also alluded to the reward that would follow: two days off for the players to relax, catch up on their studies, and get away from basketball. Then he concluded: "We've done a helluva job up to this point. Tonight's game is just like taking a midterm exam. Only tonight, we're not going to flunk it like we did last year."

With a quick prayer and that thought in mind, the Irish took the court.

The scoreless game didn't last long. With only 28 seconds gone Anatoli Mishkin hit a jump hook to put the Soviets in the lead. Bill Hanzlik answered with two free throws, but the Soviets surged ahead 8–2 and then 24–12. The first thirteen minutes belonged to the visitors as they established a 30–17 lead. The international rules and untimely turnovers began to cost the Irish on the scoreboard. Despite the bulge, Digger stuck to the script he and his assistants had prepared earlier in the week, resting the starters for a spurt the last seven minutes of the half. It couldn't have been planned any better as Notre Dame threw Gomelsky's press back at him, outscoring the Soviets, 19–6, before the behemoth Vladimir Tkachenko dropped in an easy basket following a long pass from Sergei Belov. At the half, the Soviets clung to a narrow 38–36 lead.

During the intermission, Phelps diagrammed a few situations on the blackboard, reinforcing the positive points of the first half. His coaching manner was noticeably different from past years. Although he still attempted to control the game, admonishing the officials and neutralizing the presence of Gomelsky on several occasions, the Irish players were obviously more relaxed—and so was their coach.

"I'm really proud of you guys and the job you're doing," said Digger. "You deserve to win, now it's going to come down to offense. Let's do it."

Obedient, the Notre Dame squad took the court and blew out the Russians in the second half. After shooting a poor 28.3 percent for the first twenty minutes, the club came alive, leading 66–60. All-America Kelly Tripucka exploded with six straight field goals sandwiched in an eight-of-nine shooting streak. The Irish had a commanding 84–71 lead before the walk-ons entered the game— and Notre Dame captured its gold medal with an impressive 86–76 victory.

"I knew Gomelsky's personality like Patton knew Rommel's," commented Digger in the postgame interview. For Digger, the game certainly meant more than an exhibition victory for his team. There was the personal rivalry between him and Gomelsky—and the memory that Gomelsky's club had embarassed the Irish at home the previous year. "Last year Alexandr used a press on us that he had never used before. He's a good coach and I really wanted to beat him."

The Olympic overtones of the game also motivated Digger privately. He wanted to prove that he and his players could compete on the international level. Kelly Tripucka and Bill Hanzlik had been passed over by the Pan-American team the summer before and that left the pair with something to prove. For Digger the game was a chance to prove his own abilities against the team favored to win the 1980 Olympics. He didn't let the chance escape.

"I guess I'd like to coach the Olympic team some year," he said, between hugs from his wife and kids after the game. "The coaching job is all politics, though. I'll never get it because I'm not in the Dean Smith clique." With Smith on the selection committee, former players and coaches of his have done pretty well in the competition for the coaching positions. Dave Gavitt, who was noticeably absent at the Irish–Soviet game, was a former aide of Smith's. Another Olympic assistant, Larry Brown, happened to be a former player of Smith's at North Carolina. The apparent politics behind the appointments disturbed Digger.

"It's like the year Abe Lemons and Bill Foster were named co-Coaches of the Year instead of Ray Meyer," he said. "Meyer has done more for college basketball than Lemons, Foster, and myself combined. Last year Ray was finally recognized, but it was a long time coming."

Digger doesn't feel too badly about being slighted by what he calls the "clique," since as great a coach as John Wooden of UCLA was never selected to coach the Olympics. "I'll never be accepted by those guys, so really I don't worry about it."

The postgame scene was a happy one. Notre Dame had won its gold medal in a domineering fashion, causing Gomelsky to refer to the Irish as bandits. For the next few games, Gomelsky managed to compare the Irish to every team the Soviets played, always concluding the other squad was better than Notre Dame. Digger didn't mind Gomelsky's comparison, though. The game had gone just the way the history books say it should. Patton beat Rommel and the good guys won.

After the game, it was time for another exchange between the two teams. Now, however, it would be on a different level.

Sergei Belov, the thirty-five-year-old guard who epitomizes basketball in the USSR, once mentioned in an interview that he collected stamps. That was in 1975, when the Soviet squad was just beginning its practice of touring the United States. Somehow, Digger stumbled onto the article and decided to strike a deal with Belov. Stamp collecting had been his own hobby since his youthful days in Beacon, New York. Despite a short lag in his interest just before taking the coaching job at Notre Dame, the hobby was resurrected in 1972, following Digger's six-and-twenty first year with the Irish. "After that kind of a season, a coach needs a lot of hobbies", he joked.

It was the special stamp series issued to commemorate the joint United States–Soviet space missions that brought the two collectors together. Digger had struck up a conversation with Belov before the game, and later Belov swapped the commemorative sheet through Olympic assistant Bill Gurthridge, who served as a messenger. That's how the friendship started between Sergei and Digger, and despite the battle the two teams had waged on the court earlier, it was a time to forget each other's cultural differences and relax in Digger's living room.

Sergei had come prepared for the gift exchange. A vintage bottle of Russian vodka, a scarf depicting the 1980 Olympics in Moscow, and a jar of caviar were presented to the Phelps family. But that was only half the show. What followed looked like Christmas in November: United States duck-hunting stamps, postage stamps, bourbon, golf shirts, and even one of Digger's personalized sweaters—with gold shovel insignia—were given to Sergei. And what would all that paraphernalia be without a leather shoulder bag in which to carry it back to Russia? Like two kids swapping grab-bag gifts in school, Digger and Sergei nursed a couple of Pabst beers and explained the significance behind the presents and how they reflected their countries' cultural backgrounds. Digger's wife, Terry, and the Phelps children sat and listened. Karen, the oldest of the Phelps clan, compared her father to Sergei and kidded about how Digger would fare playing basketball against college kids at age thirty-eight. After all, Sergei was thirty-five and a member of the Red Army, too. But Karen added, "I don't think Daddy could cut it playing against college kids."

Later Digger took his visitor out on the town, treating Sergei to pizza at Giuseppe's while the pair talked about the drug problem in the United States and alcoholism in Russia. Belov's tour continued to one of South Bend's disco night spots, and finished up at Notre Dame's Senior Bar. Digger loves to mix with the students whenever possible, and the Senior Bar was the perfect place to show Sergei American college life. To Digger's surprise, Sergei held his own on the dance floor as the pair ventured bravely into the disco layout with a pair of willing coeds. "You didn't learn that in Russia," chuckled Digger as he watched his guest dancing.

Fortunately for Belov his team wasn't scheduled to travel to Indiana University until late the next morning. The old friends parted, with Digger promising to visit Sergei in Russia sometime soon. Swapping stamps had provided a bond between the pair that wiped out differences between a communist and a capitalist, at least for a while. Regardless of politics, people could be people.

3

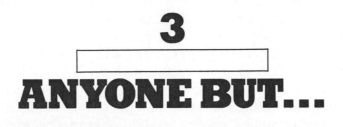

ANYONE BUT...

It didn't take long for everything that Digger and the coaching staff had built in the preseason period to come crumbling down. Just five days after the Irish had dominated the Russians, an injury that first appeared minor left the coaches shaking their heads in disbelief. A simple attempted blocked shot left Billy Hanzlik with a separated index finger on his left hand. It was a step backwards for the coaching staff.

When trainer Skip Meyer broke the news to Digger, the head coach was dressing for a speaking engagement before the Knights of Columbus in Elkhart. When the word "surgery" was mentioned, the seriousness of the injury became apparent. Hanzlik's finger was so badly dislocated that the bone had become wrapped in the ligaments of the hand. The doctors had tried every means possible to relax the ligaments, but it was a hopeless cause. Surgery was the only answer.

Suddenly Digger's manner turned from casual to a blend of intense concern that bordered on rage. Hanzlik had been the key to the victory over the Soviet team and was the cornerstone of future success for Notre Dame. Meyer, a rookie trainer, quickly learned of the pressures that sometimes go with the job. Digger demanded a second opinion, clinging to the possibility that surgery and the six-week layoff for Hanzlik might be avoided. "If it was a life-and-death emergency, where would the other doctor be?" he asked when the second surgeon couldn't be reached immediately by phone. "I want a second opinion before he's cut."

Meanwhile assistant coaches Tommy McLaughlin and Danny Nee had returned from their after-practice run to hear the bad news. Digger estimated the loss would render the majority of their planned defenses useless: Hanzlik's defensive ability made the team go; without him there would be a void. Nee agreed. "I'd rather lose any other player—Jackson, Tripucka, Branning, anyone but Hanzlik," he said.

Despite the bad news, Digger trudged on to his engagement with the Elkhart K of C. It was a cocktail hour, and the members were anxious to ask for autographs, talk about the season, and pose with Digger for a picture. The worries, the day, the practice, the injury, were suddenly left behind. Digger was among Irish fans and they couldn't be disappointed.

It started like a Johnny Carson monologue, a series of one-liners that warmed up the crowd after a home-made spaghetti dinner. Digger loved to talk to crowds. "You listen better than my players," he said. "Go ahead eating. If you want seconds, fine. But if you want thirds, I'll be gone."

This engagement was like going to any other K of C, Rotary, or VFW dinner. It was—and is—part of the coaching job at Notre Dame. The appealing aspect for Digger that night was that he could speak, have a good time, and then stop by a friends place later. There would be no plane connections or waiting in terminals. He wasn't slowing down on the circuit, he explained, just playing the dinner spots closer to home.

That night the playing included quite a routine, from answering the standard questions about the schedule and the outlook to expressing opinions on world crises, to an usher who died suddenly after thirty-five years working at Notre Dame's home games and concerts. "If there's one thing that has to come out of tonight," said Digger, "remember that there's a lot to be thankful for in our lives." With Thanksgiving a few days away, Digger mentioned the hostages in Iran who wouldn't be home with their families, and the thousands of starving Cambodians who weren't as well fed as the gathering that night. "Take it from an undertaker's son," he said, "the world today is so hyper and computerized that it doesn't let you get away from it. Don't worry about the greener pastures later; you have to unwind and get out of the rat race for a while sometime. The only way you're going to lose the game is if you beat yourself," stated Digger.

Spoken with a feeling that everyone in the room could understand, Digger had typically given more than was bargained for when the dinner was arranged. But that was Digger, anxious to espouse his feelings and philosophy to people who wanted to listen. He really believes in getting away from it for a while, cherishing the special moments. And he honestly wanted to share a little bit of his secret with others. That's one of the things he likes most about his speaking engagements—the chance to relate personally to the fans who make the Notre Dame following one of the biggest in the world.

Certainly it is not the prying questions and the attempts to unearth a controversy or a shortcoming that appeal to him. During the 1978–79 season, many people thought Digger substituted too frequently, not giving his players a chance to become accustomed to the game situation. That's a question that always pops up, along with questions about Bobby Knight and playing a soft schedule. At the K of C that night, there was even a curt remark by a man with whom Digger had spent some time reminiscing before the dinner. Digger was building to the answer of the man's question about Bobby Knight and discipline, when the man interjected, "That wasn't my question." Before he finished, Digger wound up diagramming the statement so that the man could see how his background related to his question. Sometimes, that goes with the job as well.

. After the dinner, Digger's main objective was to get to a more private phone and check on Hanzlik's condition, so he drove to a restaurant owned by Ralph Montagano, a good friend. The news was bad. Billy had been operated on and was in the recovery room. Despite the setback, Digger was glad to see Montagano, a man he admires despite some unusual circumstances. Montagano had once been arrested in a gambling raid near South Bend, a matter that concerned many people. But Digger chose to look beyond the incident. "When you look at the world today, there are certainly more pressing problems than gambling," he said to a friend as he drove back to South Bend. "How can anyone be so concerned with gambling when it's legal in one state and illegal in another? Ralph and I never discuss the spread on a game or anything related to betting on sports. It doesn't belong in athletics, that's for sure. But Ralph is a good man and I appreciate him for being himself."

Later that night, Digger also plotted his strategy for practice the following day. "I've got to turn this negative into a positive," he said. "That means that everyone will have to carry their own weight from now on—no more relying on Billy Hanzlik." Digger now was back at work mentally, forgetting about the dinner and the drink with Montagano. He prepared for what he would say to his men in the locker room. He would tell them it would take extra effort from each player and that they had to contribute right away. In a sense, he looked on the situation as an opportunity to develop his players more quickly, forcing them to stop relying on others and to play the role that was required of each of them.

"That's what I'll do tomorrow," he said. "We'll listen to some music and then I'll tell them this is it. It's back to the beginning. There's no Hanzlik to fall back on. If they want to succeed as a team, now's the time to start."

And that was his exact message the next day. "Billy Hanzlik meant as much to us defensively as Magic Johnson meant to Michigan State offensively," he said. The team was gathered to watch the Russian game film, to see what they had done right and where they could improve. More significantly, however, it was time to turn Hanzlik's injury into something positive. But before the squad would be ready for this, Digger the psychologist had to go to work. Quietly, he explained just what had happened since Hanzlik left practice the day before. The players were silent as they heard that Billy would be in a cast for three weeks, missing the UCLA game— but hopefully back on the team in time for the Kentucky game on December 29. Digger rattled off a list of defenses that revolved around Hanzlik's aggressiveness: the full, three-quarter, and half-court presses, man to man, whatever. But without letting the team know how big a blow the loss meant to the coaching plans, Digger started building confidence again, telling the team it didn't need Hanzlik to win.

"There's enough talent in this room, no matter what injuries or foul troubles develop in a game, that we can still go out and play and win." He spoke of the front-line players concentrating even harder on their roles, defense and rebounding. For the backcourt, he told the four guards they must wear their opponents down and play more aggressive defense. "You're going to have to talk to each other now because Billy won't be there to do the talking for you," he reminded them. Then he mentioned a new element into his coaching style in this, his tenth year as a college head coach. He promised the team he'd try to tone down his pugnacity a bit. "The old man is getting a little mellow," he said hopefully.

Then he asked, "Is there anything anybody wants to talk about before we watch the Russian films and see what we can get out of it?" Silence. "All right, let's get to it."

4

THE
RECRUITING TRAIL

Following practice, Digger and Danny Nee didn't have much time to worry about how practice looked, or about the reaction of the team to the loss of Hanzlik. The pair headed for Fort Wayne, an Indiana town less than two hours south of Notre Dame. They had been working hard with the players already on the team, but after practice it was time to start looking for Irish players of the future. Digger and Nee were hitting the recruiting trail. Their day was only half over.

Notre Dame had its eye on a senior from Harding High School, 6-foot-4 guard Jim Master. According to an assessment by Nee, Master could be the answer to their graduation losses at the end of the season. Master's shooting abilities were highly touted, with a junior-season field-goal percentage of .571; this, coupled with a school-record forty consecutive free throws, backed up his reputation. Nee was bringing Digger to see the ballhandler first-hand, knowing that if Digger liked the player he'd offer him a grant-in-aid on the spot.

And Nee was optimistic. "I'm sure you'll like Jim tonight," he told Digger. "He can shoot, he's a floor general, and he's got the grades to make it academically at Notre Dame." As Digger headed his car down a rural state road that wound through a strip of scenic farmland, the pair outlined their strategy, talking about the points they should raise with Master that night. According to NCAA rules, the coaches were allowed a "bump," the chance to run into the player and his parents before or after a game. In a short time, the coaches would have to cover a lot of ground, and they weighed the proper approach.

"We're losing our two starting guards to graduation, so Jim knows he'll have a chance to play," Digger reminded Nee. "He's a smart kid. What we have to do is reassert our interest, make our commitment to him for four years, and talk about the university."

Recruiting pits one school against another, and often the high school senior is swayed by a glamorous sales pitch that may not be all true. Despite the backstabbing that often goes on, Digger refuses to follow negative recruiting practices that degrade another school's program. He is a positive recruiter, one who feels that Notre Dame has enough of its own to offer without having to criticize other schools. If Notre Dame can't stand up in the eyes of the recruit, chances are the recruit would be unhappy there and that's when Digger throws in the towel. When he's sure all the facts are understood and a recruit has the necessary information to make a mature decision, Digger withdraws.

Sometimes, though, Digger admits that it's necessary to open a player's eyes with hard facts about what he'd be passing up by not attending Notre Dame. "There are situations when a senior in high school might be naive about something or unable to make the right decision for himself," he explains. "That's when you have to appeal to his parents, to try to make sure he doesn't make a choice that he'll regret later."

When the pair arrived at the Northrup High School gym, Digger entered unobtrusively by the back door, thanks to the help of the school's football coach, a Notre Dame graduate who had played for Frank Leahy; it was a little luck of the Irish the two stumbled on. There were passes at the front door, but the lines and the attention were something Digger could do without at that time. The Notre Dame coaches stayed in the upper level of the stands, where they could be in the background, quite a contrast to Eldon Miller of Ohio State, Lee Rose of Purdue, Joe B. Hall of Kentucky, and a Vanderbilt assistant coach. That contingent was seated right behind press row and the scoring table, plainly visible to Master throughout the game. The principal of the school also invited Digger and Nee to join the other coaches, but Digger demurred, thanking the principal for his courtesy, but saying he was okay in the stands. "I don't have to be the center of attention at a high school game," he later explained. "Although some people think I have an ego that requires a fanfare or something, I don't like to steal the kids' show. The high school game is the attraction, not me."

Before it was over, it seemed as if every youngster in the gym found Digger's hiding place and tracked him down for an autograph. Without hesitation, the Irish coach scrawled "Digger" in his characteristic printed style. Before it was over, hundreds left the gym with the neat penmanship of Joe B., the written signature of Lee Rose, and Digger's mark.

From the time Master burst through the paper circle held by the cheerleaders to initiate the season opener, the senior played a heady game that impressed Digger. He scored thirty-four points in the win, and the college coaches lined up for their "bumps."

"You're what we're going to need at the guard position next year," Digger told Master frankly. "If you say the word, we'll stop recruiting the other guards and sign you to an institutional letter whenever you want. I guarantee that no matter what happens through four years of college, the scholarship is yours and you can come to Notre Dame and be yourself as a player and a person."

After a little chit-chat about the season the sell was over and the recruiting was done for the night. That's the way college recruiting has developed. Coaches travel long hours to spend a few minutes with a prospective player. Fortunately for Digger and Nee, there was a stop at a tavern in Bremen to look forward to on the ride back; Hoople's, a local watering hole where the "Major Hoople" comic strip started, is also home for "Tiger" and "Tank," a couple of regular customers whom Digger and Nee enjoy whenever they get together: Tank is a behemoth figure while Tiger is his smaller sidekick. On arriving, Nee walked down to the fire station to call Tip-Off Club officer, "J. R." —Duwayne Elliott—because Hoople's doesn't have a phone. After a round of beers, the pair was headed back for South Bend and on to Digger's Lake Michigan home for a Thanksgiving Day meal. Digger laughed about the stop at Hoople's all the way back. He and Nee had left their ties in the bar at the request of Tiger and Tank. The Hoople's contingent had been invited to sit behind the bench for the Valparaiso game by Danny. It was one of the moments Digger says he stays at Notre Dame to enjoy.

Many coaches might not trust their assistants enough to leave them to run practice on the day before the home opener, but that was exactly what Digger was doing, and his absence displayed the confidence he had in his assistants' abilities. It was Friday afternoon and Digger, overcoat and briefcase in hand, was walking out of the office on his way to Slater, Missouri. He paused in the outer office and joked with Danny Nee. "Don't screw it up," he said. "If we lose to Valpo tomorrow it won't look good when I tell the press you prepared the team." As Digger turned toward the door Nee needled his boss back, saying "Bye, Diggie," and waving his arm much as his own little son, Patrick, would. Digger knew Nee could handle a head-coaching job, let alone a practice. In fact, Digger hoped Danny would get his chance after that season. It was his time to move on.

There were brief stops at the Administration Building, where Digger carried out one of his pregame rituals—walking through the Development Office and asking the secretaries to get out their rosaries in preparation for the home contest. He whirled through the maze of dividers that separated their desks, pausing for a quip or a laugh with the women. "Get down to the Grotto and say those Hail Marys," he told them.

He also made a brief stop in Jim Gibbons's office to tell him about the trip to Slater, where he would get another chance to see Joe Kleine, a 6-foot-11, 240-pound center. Jim was a great basketball fan who also refereed high school games and provided color commentary for WCFL radio in Chicago at many Irish contests. Then Digger was off to the airport to meet his friend Pete Pilliod, and take off for Slater in the comfort of Pete's private plane.

Flying isn't one of Digger's favorite pastimes. He figured that with as much traveling as he does in the course of a season the odds might catch up with him sometime. He and the team had already had a recent close call. One night the entire Evansville, Indiana basketball team had been killed when its DC–3 crashed. Notre Dame had been supposed to use the same DC–3 to return from Bloomington, but foggy conditions had forced Digger to opt for a bus trip instead. The Federal Aviation Association investigation of the crash indicated that the pilot had forgotten to remove a block that locked the tail rudder in place while the plane was parked so that wind would not whip it around. "Three people missed taking it out and when the pilot got his plane airborne he found he couldn't steer the aircraft," Digger remarked. From that point on, he had always checked with the pilots about removing the block. And now, as he climbed aboard Pete's plane, Digger checked again. "You've got a great pilot," he told Pete. "He probably feels insulted when I ask him that." With that the pair sat back and caught up on each other's activities as Pete reached into the refrigerator for a couple of beers. Pete had been to Slater once before, to see Joe Kleine, and had enjoyed the trip so much that he had volunteered the plane's service to go again. He wasn't disappointed after this jaunt, either.

A pair of Irish loyalists—Frank Markovich and Walter "Shorty" Haines—met Digger at Marshall Airport. It was ironic that Digger, the son of an undertaker, would be guided around the small town by none other than the town undertaker and the local pharmacist. "I should have picked you up in the hearse, Digger," laughed Shorty as the group headed for the Haineses' apartment above the funeral parlor. Their wives had prepared a pheasant dinner with all the trimmings, topped off with a shot of Wild Turkey liqueur for good measure.

Digger knew the entire Kleine family would not be at the game. Joe's father had just had a scare after a local doctor told him he might be suffering from a heart problem. Fortunately, a cardiologist's examination turned up nothing, but that night, on doctor's orders, the father would miss his son's opening game. The sincerity of Joe's parents touched Phelps. Recruiting Joe had been a pleasure for him because of the easy manner and directness the Kleines conveyed. Digger was looking forward to seeing Joe lead his team against Marshall, their big rival from the next town. The small gymnasium was packed and Kleine didn't disappoint his team, the townspeople, or Digger. The powerful young man poured in thirty-four points and grabbed twenty-nine rebounds as his long arms snared every loose ball in sight. Digger kept nudging Pete throughout the contest, likening Joe to Indiana University star center Kent Benson, whom he had also recruited. "Just give me Joe Kleine, Tim Andree, and Tom Sluby up front and we'll be awesome," he predicted. Phelps waited until the Slater team straggled from the locker room, then spent a few minutes with Kleine, while several other coaches waited for their turn. Digger advised Joe he was just the player for the Irish and counseled him not to worry about making his mind up in the next few days.

Although Kleine had impressed Digger, Missouri coach Norm Stewart was also chasing the quiet young man. Stewart had captured Steve Stepanovich, a St. Louis star, the year before; now he had called on state officials and businessmen to write Kleine letters urging the young man to stay in the state and choose Missouri as Stepanovich had. Digger knew Stewart's tactics from the recruiting war over Stepanovich the year before, but he had declined to get into a mail campaign with the rival. An hour later Pete's plane was heading for South Bend with two happy recruiters enjoying the flight. Digger was confident Joe Kleine would come to Notre Dame.

5

GETTING IT GOING

Granted, the Valparaiso Crusaders were not the opening challenge that Maryland presented Notre Dame in 1976. The Irish held a 21–1 series advantage, the only loss dating back to 1921, the early years of Notre Dame basketball.

Still, the Crusaders constituted the first hurdle for the Irish. Within seven days Digger's club would face four teams in rapid succession: Valparaiso, Dec. 1; Iowa State, Dec. 3; Northwestern, Dec. 5; and St. Louis, Dec. 8. These were the contests in which Notre Dame would develop a pattern for the season, get in the groove for the months ahead. Notre Dame could shake off the cobwebs against Valparaiso and begin to develop a playing style and team character without Billy Hanzlik. There was little doubt in Phelps's mind. The chemistry he desired had been present in the Russian game. The club had reacted well to the challenge it faced from a team of near-professionals. Now, with an important ingredient missing, the formula would have to be adjusted and retested for at least six weeks. Following the season opener, the pace would gradually build against an Iowa State team billed as "the tallest college team in the country." The front line would be pressed hardest and Orlando Woolridge would be baptized at the new center position. St. Louis was also waiting in the wings to ambush the Irish on the A.C.C. court. The Billikens would gladly upset Notre Dame, hoping to catch the Irish looking ahead to the annual extravaganza at home against the UCLA Bruins.

Digger would have to deal with these challenges as he eased his club into the college basketball season. On the night of the season opener, he was ready to submerge himself in the tempest, surfacing occasionally through the next four months for brief breaths of fresh air.

Valparaiso coach Ken Rochlitz quickly learned that the Irish were worthy of their top-ten ranking. An eight-point outburst before a capacity crowd at the center let everyone know the regular season was under way. Tripucka, Jackson, Branning, and Woolridge capitalized quickly on offensive chances. All four "regulars" hit from the floor in the first three minutes to establish the 8–0 lead. Orlando's basket was especially pleasing as Tracy went with a behind-the-back pass to send the "Tree" on his way for a fast-break slam dunk—a shot Orlando cherishes and the crowd loves.

Digger allowed the starters ten minutes of uninterrupted play as the quintet went ahead of the outmanned visitors, 20–8. Then, with the regular season only ten minutes old, a fresh wave of players entered the game for the Irish. Salinas, Mitchell, Andree, Paxson, and Varner replaced the starters, maintained the dozen-point edge they inherited, and even added three points to it before the half ended. Seeing the young players early in the season was no surprise to the Irish fans. Digger, noted for developing his bench, sent three freshmen, a sophomore, and a junior to mind the lead. If anything, the second platoon's efforts were more aggressive, as frosh Paxson led all Notre Dame scorers at the half with ten points.

The A.C.C. crowd was treated to another strong half of Irish basketball, and at the end, the only question that remained was whether Digger's team would hit the hundred-point mark. Usually that feat is in the hands of the walk-ons who appear late in the contest when the outcome is assured. But this was the first time Digger had to run some different defenses without Hanzlik in the key role. He took advantage of the opportunity and stayed with the first ten players. Although some spectators might have thought that he was running up the score, this was not the case. It was part of the conditioning and experience Digger felt his team needed as it prepared for the Bruins.

Finally, with a half-minute left, Hawkins, Kelly, and Healy entered the game. Notre Dame breezed to its first victory with a 92–66 win. Still, in the press conference that followed, little would be made of the team effort as writers searched for Notre Dame's Achilles heel.

Digger was pleased with the victory, the play of the starters, and freshman John Paxson's dozen points and two assists. "I thought there were periods where we played very well, and because of those situations we were able to get our young players into the game," he said. "These kids need confidence. We have to show the young players that the coaches believe in them so they'll be ready to play whenever we need them." A writer remarked that at times their effort seemed inconsistent, when the twenty-five point lead sometimes slipped to fourteen. That was the last thing Digger had on his mind. Tim Andree had gone five for six, finishing with thirteen points, Paxson had a dozen points, while Varner was shut out. The freshman from Pittsburgh felt the pressure a little more in his first game, having had to cope with a noisy 11,345 spectators—who included his parents. Digger figured privately that this might have had something to do with Bill's 0 for 5 shooting performance. "They all go through that," he said. "Bill was a little tight but he'll come through it."

"Lack of concentration" on the part of Woolridge was the point of the next question. Digger took the pressure off Woolridge by noting that Valparaiso's strong play in the middle earned them some points. "Let's give Valpo some credit there," Digger said. "It was a low post play and Orlando fronted his man instead of playing behind him. Still, I think Orlando was awesome on the boards, and that's his role this year."

Sometimes, no matter what the outcome or margin of victory, it's not enough at Notre Dame. Winning and winning big is something the fans take for granted and the media carping after a twenty-six–point victory bears the theory out.

"This is the thing about this basketball team," said Digger, setting the tone for the year. "I don't think people can expect them to go out and be awesome for an entire forty minutes; the game just isn't played that way anymore. You go out and look for spurts to get it done. We kept our poise and knew we were going to win. We weren't out to prove we can win by forty points." He went on to remind the press of the ninety-two–point offensive performance and the sixty-six–point defensive effort. "What more can I say?" He wrapped it up with some praise for the Valparaiso program, noting that their club was much improved from the previous year. "They should feel good about some of the things they're doing." It was sincere praise. Digger has had to go through building programs too.

The Valparaiso experience actually continued on Sunday when the team convened for its first postgame practice. After watching the films Digger put the players through some drills to correct weaknesses and shortcomings he had pointed out on the screen. By reacting to recent game situations in drills the players would learn how to react in future contests and the extra practice would add more consistency to the team's play. Sticking to a structured timetable, he worked on defensive rebounding, baseline penetration, ball watching, and execution of the press offense and defense. Five minutes would be spent on each element, and then a student manager would remind Digger it was time to move on.

Then they prepared for their next challenge, Iowa State, a Big Eight team that boasted a front line of 6-foot-6, 6-foot-9, and 6-foot-11 players. If the Irish were to be successful, it would take finesse in front, crashing the boards on the offensive, and a pressure defense that would wear the other team down and cause turnovers.

"We've got four ball games in the next eight days and it's time to put it together this week," Digger pointed out in the first of two pregame talks to the team. "Your strength will be tested by their size and you'd better be ready." He also drew the team's attention by guessing what was being said in the visitors' locker room. They're in there thinking about how to play you," he said. "They're probably thinking of taking it at you in the post areas because you're weak on post defense and you're not consistent yet. I'd crash the offensive boards because you're doing too much ball watching when the other team shoots. I'd also take it to you in fast-break situations or in press offense because you're not getting back and somebody is going to be open. Those are the weaknesses I would have detected if I was Lynn Nance [the Iowa coach] and I watched the Valparaiso game."

It was simple and to the point, an alarm to wake up the club after playing a relatively easy opponent. Forget the articles and last game's box score. It's a new forty minutes tonight. Digger outlined the game plan, urging the team to "trust the defense and remember what we taught you yesterday." He knew the front line would be tested, and he had worked with the forwards to help equalize their height disadvantage. "Go to your man on defensive rebounding situations" he said, "and if he's bigger than you and reaching over your back go to him a step sooner so he can't go over you. That will neutralize his jumping ability." The same defensive ploy had worked against the taller Russians and Digger warned his team not to get caught directly under the basket. Instead, they should go out to the dotted line of the circular foul-shooting area.

Digger reiterated the essential points he thought the team had to concentrate on to beat Iowa State. He tried to keep things simple and precise. His pregame pattern is to go through the detailed strategy in the first talk, saving a brief refresher and one of his patented fiery pep talks for the second locker-room meeting about ten minutes before introductions. The pattern held through on this night, as he sent them out to the game with the final direction, "Show them what the game of basketball is all about."

That didn't exactly happen in the first twenty minutes of play. Iowa State was giving the Irish fits on the boards, trailing by only seven points at the half. Tracy Jackson and Bill Varner were the only two players to manage offensive rebounds, and defensively Orlando and Kelly Tripucka were not playing up to their abilities. John Paxson was also having a tough time, guarding a much quicker guard. Digger was not happy with the team's offensive execution and he let them know about it. Manager Stacy Russo told the team they had shot sixteen for thirty, and Digger said they should have been shooting 65 percent and be leading by twenty if they had had more offensive rebounds. "It's not there and we're not ready, mentally," he said. "Believe me, that's not UCLA out there; the Bruins are really playing and you have to face them next week. If you want the headlines to read 'Iowa State Upsets Notre Dame' keep playing like this. Show me, don't talk about something, show me. You better kick some butt or you're going to be embarrassed.

The team capitalized on a couple of spurts, winning by ten points, 87–77.

Digger was pleased with that part of the game, but it was the determination and character of John Paxson that impressed him most. "Paxson had a bad first half, but came back in the second half and played himself out of it," he said. "A few mistakes don't worry me; it's when you make the mistakes and then forget your role on the team and start to worry about your ego." But this hadn't happened to his freshman guard, said Digger. "A freshman stunk out the place in the first half, and he knew it; but he couldn't wait to play and play hard in the second half. If you're in a slump, you listen to me and play out of it. If you have a problem, come and talk to me alone. When one kid can do it, that means everyone should be able to do it. And if you're weak on defense, admit it. That team shouldn't have had seventy-seven points."

Digger went on to tell Tripucka how he'd got eaten up by Bob Estes, a 6-foot-11 forward for the Cyclones. "Orlando, you too. I told you how to play Uthoff and the first time he gets the ball you go for his head fake and he scores. Did you watch the back of his numbers like I told you, stay back a foot when he had the ball? If you did, you wouldn't have been sucked in and embarrassed." To stress this, Digger also outlined Tim Andree's defensive play against Uthoff—how Andree followed instructions and succeeded.

After landing on Tripucka and Woolridge for poor defense, Digger then encouraged freshman Bill Varner who had failed to score his first hoop again tonight. It wasn't all encouragement, though. "Billy, you must be the sickest kid on campus," said Digger. "You're slumping, but you listen to me and I'll bring you through it. Don't listen to other people because you'll go deeper and deeper. You're a hell of a player and I want you to come up, not slip deeper."

Digger also went into strategy and other matters. "I was trying to pull out all kinds of plays tonight because I was worried about Iowa State," he said. "They were a good basketball team with experienced players. Billy Hanzlik isn't around now to save your tails defensively; you have to be aware of these things." Hanzlik sat quietly in the locker room, wishing he could have been out there helping his club. Shortly after, Billy was drawn into the discussion when Digger made a plea for the team to respond to him. He was trying his best not to yell and get on individuals, something that he sometimes does without thinking in the heat of a game. Hanzlik affirmed that Digger was doing his best, and that it was up to the members of the team to begin to respond to the mental aspects of the game.

"I'm telling you the truth, you're not ready to play UCLA," Digger shouted. "I've seen the films, so listen to the man. The man is getting mellow, but he knows what he's talking about. I've changed and made a commitment but some of you aren't listening or concentrating."

The team bowed their heads as Digger led the men in a postgame prayer. Then he said, "We have to work and you'd better dedicate yourselves because that's the only way to get it done."

It was obvious from the films that Northwestern was a good basketball team despite their reputation as the perennial Big Ten doormat. The Wildcats were coming off a horrendous season, one where everything that could have gone wrong did. Coach Rich Falk suffered through his first season at Northwestern with a 6–21 record. Now, the scouting reports indicated that Falk had landed three outstanding freshmen to go with three returning starters and eight returning lettermen overall. Playing the Wildcats in Chicago at ancient McGaw Hall did not thrill Digger.

Certainly he did not want the team to be distracted by the crowd and the different surroundings. For the freshmen, this was another hurdle. Paxson, Andree, and Varner would get their first playing experience on the road. Fortunately, however, McGaw Hall was almost equally divided between Northwestern fans and Notre Dame's Chicago alumni. The graduates and subway alumni group had once again turned out to support their favorites.

"You've got to play tonight against a team that is your equal mentally," Digger warned as he addressed the team before they took the floor. "Northwestern's academic standards are outstanding. The difference will be your talent; if you concentrate and execute, you'll win. I want an aggressive game from you tonight, right from the very start. The starters have eight minutes to get it going, I want a big spurt where you guys really push yourselves. Then, we've got to let our bench get involved; that's their role and I want them ready to play."

The game plan was taking shape as Digger continued. "Now there's seven minutes left and I want another key move; I want to see the intensity when you turn it on again. Then, with three minutes left you guys should end the game, not going from a twelve-point lead to a six, but from a twelve lead to a twenty." Digger had written the script. Now it was up to the team to try to act it out. Concentration, intensity, and rebounding were again the key elements that Digger wanted to get across to his players.

At first the team let the little things get in the way, playing tentatively as they adjusted to the surroundings. Several times a player complained to an official about fouls that slipped by uncalled. But then the team finally settled down into the flow that Digger had outlined and the pattern began to develop as the Irish reserve strength wore down the Wildcats. The margin at the half was ten points, 35–25. Digger was pleased with the progress.

"Don't complain about not getting foul shots," were his first words at halftime. "You tried it for twenty minutes and it didn't work; you're not going to get a call. So what do you do? You go out and play well, which is what you're doing."

Notre Dame's defense had been especially effective, forcing the home team to shoot .321 from the floor in the first twenty minutes. The Irish also didn't give up a transition basket, a success attributed to the players coming back quickly to pick up their men. Digger reviewed the success of his multiple defenses as the managers reported those defenses the Wildcats had scored against.

"You're doing a helluva job," Digger told the team. "It's your first road game of the year and you're up by ten at halftime. A couple of calls went against us; embarrassing calls went against us. There were a few easy points given up, and we're not getting offensive rebounds. But overall, you're doing what I want."

Later in the halftime break Billy Hanzlik approached Digger with an offensive alignment that he thought might work, and before the half expired Digger was up at the chalkboard diagramming it for the team. "Pay attention to this. Hanzlik pointed this out and I think it's a hell of an idea." Hanzlik was still in street clothes, but the involved senior was still trying to help the team in whatever way he could. It pleased Digger that his captain could pick up an offense that might work, that floor leadership ability would be forthcoming so soon.

Northwestern shot better in the second half, but still only managed a .458 percentage and wound up the game with a dismal field goal mark of .385. The Irish pulled away from the Wildcats, but not without some moments of concern. Kelly Tripucka collided with a Northwestern player and tumbled off the elevated court floor. Fortunately he was all right, but it was still an anxious moment for the coaches. Digger cleared the bench with a minute left and the walk-ons made a rare appearance in an away game. Hawkins and Kelly don't travel with the team like senior walk-on Tim Healy, who Digger believes has earned the trips. The only thing that didn't go right was Billy Varner's continued drought; he went 0 for 3 in two minutes of play.

Digger had some brief comments after the game, noting that the defensive pressure was developing and that more fruitful practice sessions would help that area. Notre Dame's next opponent would be St. Louis on Saturday night, three days away. That wasn't what Digger was worried about, though.

"St. Louis is coming up Saturday, but I'm going to be honest with you," he said. "Tomorrow we start working on UCLA; we've got to get the groundwork in because they're going to play you as aggressively as you've ever seen anyone play. Larry Brown is a great defensive coach working with some of the same personnel you saw last year. Yes, we play St. Louis at home Saturday; we're not going to lose to them, either. But we're gunning for the Bruins at home because they embarrassed us at home last year. I want the mental edge that you had tonight and against the Russians. We can win Saturday and Tuesday."

Digger also mentioned Varner's continuing slump, calling on the other members of the "basketball family" to pump him up. "You guys have been through it before, give Billy some support." Then, turning to Varner he said, "All I can say is that Toby Knight only played eighty-seven minutes as a freshman, Billy. Now he's starting for the New York Knicks of the NBA. Just be patient and wait your chance—the shots will fall."

Tomorrow afternoon it would be back to work preparing for the Bruins, they were told, and Digger wanted the team to begin to prepare mentally. It was Tripucka's job to pick the music selection for the first Bruin practice. "Let's get out of here in thirty-five minutes and get back to South Bend early," said Digger. "That means Rich will have to take a cab, he'll never get ready in a half-hour." Unfortunately, Branning wasn't the only one that slowed the club's return to school. The bus driver got lost, turning a two-and-a-half hour trip into a five-hour ordeal. It was a tired group by the time the Golden Dome became visible.

As the team ate its pregame meal at the South Dining Hall on campus, Digger was occupied with St. Louis *Globe-Democrat* reporter Joe Castellano. Despite the rumors of steak dinners and other extravagances heaped on Notre Dame athletes, the basketball team occupied three tables in the empty dining hall while workers and part-time students were getting ready for the dinner rush. The meal was equally undistinguished: do-it-yourself bacon-lettuce-and-tomato sandwiches.

Digger gobbled his way through the meal, all the time talking with the reporter about his coaching ideas and philosophies. This kind of interview is common for Digger during a season. The colorful coach is what is known as "a good interview" in press circles. He says the right things. He's got his own views and expresses them regardless of what college basketball coaches are "supposed" to say. Digger makes good copy.

It was obvious that Castellano had done some homework. His questions went beyond the usual game-by-game strategy. He drew a connection between the great increase in college basketball popularity and Digger's coaching career in the early 1970's and added that both occurrences coincided with the demise of UCLA. Digger declined, between mouthfuls of a B.L.T., to take credit for the increased popularity of the game. The sandwich was less of a mouthful than the analogy and easier to swallow, too. "Since Lew Alcindor left UCLA there's been an influx of big men into the game," he noted. "That's made college basketball very competitive, every team you play has a 6-foot-11 or 7-footer. The post-Korean War population boom was great for the game and when Duke emphasized national recruiting, it caught on. Now everyone is recruiting at high school games and summer camps."

Eventually the discussion got around to the marketing aspects of college basketball. Double-headers on Sunday television are commonplace now, and Notre Dame's involvement in that marketing growth was apparent.

"A few years ago we appeared on national TV quite a few times on Saturdays and Sundays because we were the first team to go out and start scheduling conference teams on their days off," Digger recalled. "We received quite a few complaints and a lot of people were upset because NBC televised Notre Dame–UCLA or Notre Dame–Michigan. Of course, a lot of the conferences are following our leads, now.

"We played Michigan in the Silverdome before 37,000 fans and I think basketball arenas of the future will be that big," Digger predicted. "I wouldn't go out today and build one with less than 30,000 seats. The University of Michigan's football stadium seats 105,000 people and they break attendance records every year.

Whoever built it forty years ago had a great idea. His concept of college football and the marketing opportunities was right on."

Somehow Phelps always gets around to talking about football. Despite his success on the hardcourt, deep down Digger is a frustrated football coach. He suggested that professional sports have begun to pay more attention to the success of the college game.

"The NFL is starting to market pro football like the college game," said Digger. "Two years ago there was Denver's 'Orange Crush,' a gimmick that drew the fans to the team. Now professional fans all over the country are waving pom-poms at games and cheering like it's their alma mater. Spirit like that keeps it all healthy."

When Castellano probed Digger about his feelings on professional basketball, Digger compared college and pro rules in football and basketball. In football, he said, the rules are almost identical. It's virtually the same game. But in pro basketball, the rules are like night and day: "It's almost as if it's not the same game being played." The reporter likened the NBA to a Broadway production, with a star or soloist grabbing all the attention. "That goes back to the rules, the mechanics that regulate pro basketball," said Digger. "The pros don't even throw the ball up to start the game; they take it out of bounds instead. The fans think that's too mechanical; it's stereotyped and there's no creativity or strategy. If there is strategy, it's too difficult for the fan to comprehend."

Digger had to break off the interview for a few minutes as he quickly ran through some game films with the team in a corner of the dining hall. When he returned he jokingly reminded Castellano: "That was St. Louis, not UCLA."

The discussion of the college basketball scene continued with an appraisal of coaching styles. "I think you have to look at what you are first as a person, and then you have to emulate your personality in your coaching," said Digger. "Whatever you are as a person you have to be as a coach. If you copy John Wooden and your team gets behind by a dozen points you can't get on a phone and say, 'Hey John, what now?'"

The interview wound down with Digger explicitly targeting his goal for the team—the NCAA championship game. He spelled it out. "We've done it all before. The only thing left is to win it." There was no room for speculation; the team's goal was clear and measuring its final achievement would be something anyone could do.

After the interview Digger went to Sacred Heart Church, where he slipped through the mass that was going on in the main church to the back altar. He was working on a novena, a series of prayers said over several days for a special intention. His prayers were directed to Saint Jude, the patron saint of hopeless causes. For nine days he said the prayer, and then walked down to the Grotto where he lit a candle. "I often do this before UCLA or when things aren't going well with the team," he told a friend. UCLA had always been his game and Digger was covering all the preparations, mentally, physically, and spiritually. It wasn't that there was reason to be worried; he was pleased with the team's progress. There had also been a good sign outside his office window that morning, the appearance of a red cardinal that he considered his good luck charm. He'd need them all for the Bruins. But he also had to remember the St. Louis game was only hours away.

The most challenging aspect of the day turned out to be the interview with Castellano. The Billikens, who had beaten Digger two out of three times in previous meetings, hung close for the first fourteen minutes. Notre Dame led 30–21 and started to pull away when the officials called a foul on John Paxson. It was the team's seventh personal. The referees missed the bonus rule that should have sent a Billiken player to the line; but when they called another foul on guard Mike Mitchell forty seconds later, they realized their mistake, and chose to correct it. St. Louis now scored four straight points from the foul line. What had been a referee's error turned out to be the Billikens' downfall. Digger not only raged at the officials for blowing the call in the first place but used the mistake to ignite his club. The offensive and defensive effort that followed was awesome. St. Louis had trailed by only four points, 31–27, with 5:21 left in the first half. But when the horn sounded to end the half, Notre Dame had reeled off twenty-two points while shutting out the visitors for the first half's remainder. It was the spurt that Digger wanted. It put his team ahead 53–27.

The rest was history as the Irish eased up on Ron Ekker's charges, finishing with a 93–65 victory. The win was sweet, keeping Notre Dame undefeated going into the UCLA game. But the cohesion and consistency the unit displayed was what Digger was after. He was also happy and relieved for Billy Varner, who broke out of his slump with a four-for-four shooting performance. Gil Salinas also scored a career high with fourteen points as a front-line substitute. To Digger it was a good sign that the role playing he wanted was developing, "Gil and Billy just went through the ups and downs that you have to learn to deal with in college and in life," he said afterwards. "You guys have to pull each other through and remember what it's like to be down when you're on top. We've got to help each other and come together as a team and as people.

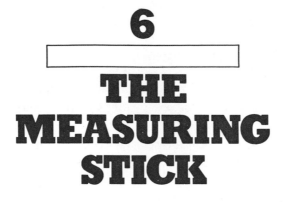

6

THE MEASURING STICK

There are three events at Notre Dame that every sports fan should experience once in his life: the epic Irish–Southern Cal football game, the Irish–Wisconsin hockey series, and the annual Notre Dame–UCLA basketball classic. Digger was getting his team ready for its moment in the spotlight.

California teams have a knack for inspiring Notre Dame, notably because of their athletic excellence. The University of California–Los Angeles was no exception. When Digger Phelps inherited the Irish basketball program from John Dee in 1971, there was only one direction to go. It was true that Dee had posted a 20–9 record the previous season with the great star of Irish basketball, Austin Carr, captaining the team. But the club that Digger inherited was a skeleton of the previous year's team. Awesome Austin graduated and so did Sid Catlett and Collis Jones. Phelps was left with Gary Novak, Tom O'Mara, and the Townsend brothers, Willie and Mike, who were on loan from Ara Parseghian's football program. The first-year coach suffered through a 6–20 year, losing to Indiana 94–29, only to be humiliated again the next game by UCLA 114–56. The next season Digger put together a respectable 18–12 season, but was still soundly beaten by John Wooden's Bruins, who were overpowering college basketball with win after win, season after season. The Irish were handed double defeats as the two teams began a home and home series in which they would meet twice a season on each others' courts. The Bruins scored a 26–point victory at Pauley Pavilion and a 19–point decision in South Bend. The pattern was developing as Digger continued to reconstruct the Irish basketball program.

Finally, on January 19, 1974, Digger's Notre Dame team beat UCLA. An eighty-eight–game winning streak that will probably never again be repeated was halted when the Irish ran off twelve unanswered points in the last 3:22 of the game, clawing their way to a 71–70 win. The Notre Dame basketball program had arrived; Digger had defeated a team that stood for college basketball supremacy. He could now dismiss the two preceding seasons. UCLA was his measuring stick as he evaluated his progress, and the importance he places on the series dates back to his beginnings at Notre Dame.

Now, six years later, it was a long practice for the Irish squad on Sunday, as the coaching staff worked to run through the new alignments the game plan demanded. Digger knew he had to be hard on the kids, hounding them to pay attention to what he was trying to get across. He had been studying UCLA game videotapes even before Thanksgiving, looking for new wrinkles that first-year coach Larry Brown might be including in the Bruin playbook. He also scrutinized Brown's personality during pregame and halftime interviews, watching the former Denver Nuggets mentor as he called plays from the bench and during time-out situations. After looking at UCLA's games against the Polish team, Digger remarked, "Two things never change at UCLA: the uniforms and the offense. It must be in the coaching contract."

Indeed, Larry Brown had not made any wholesale changes, although he was slowly sliding the team into his patterned run-and-jump defense. Not that much else had changed, including the broadcaster's references to UCLA great John Wooden. Inwardly Digger wondered if Brown would be haunted by the ghost of Wooden as previous coaches Gene Bartow and Gary Cunningham had been. That must also be a part of the job.

Digger and his assistants agreed that the strength of the Bruins would be their experienced front line of Kiki Vandeweghe, James Wilkes, and Darrell Allums. The backcourt was young and talented, but Digger hoped he could exploit that inexperience with good defense, plus the added pressure that the crowd would place on the visitors.

There were the usual signs of the impending classic. Digger's secretary, Dottie Van Paris, was so swarmed with ticket requests that she barely had time for any of her other daily duties. Dottie shielded Digger from as many of the distractions as she could because it was clear to her the boss was submerged in preparations for the game.

"You can tell it's UCLA week," said Digger, pointing out that there was always something special about this one game at the Athletic and Convocation Center. "It's not so much that I'm uptight; it's the good feeling that I have about the game, a nervousness that I really like before any UCLA game." That feeling often rubbed off on the assistants as they prepared their assignments. Tommy McLaughlin had coordinated the scouting and films, and though he had done well, Digger took over from that point; he was playing a more active role in this game than he had in others. Sometimes this extra participation and intensity added to his assistants' nervousness. That was part of the UCLA week and a part of the job.

Monday afternoon the team went through a light workout as the staff decided to lighten up after its tiring Sunday session. Tiny index cards hung over each player's locker as a reminder to keep the mental edge going. "Concentration," they said. That key element was stressed over and over. That night there was a brief pep rally as a boisterous crowd filled the auxiliary gymnasium of the A.C.C. Irish football pep rallies were a tradition, and Digger wanted it to carry over to basketball. It turned out to be a family affair, with Digger's folks in attendance along with some players' parents.

Tuesday's schedule was almost anticlimactic for Digger. He had breakfast with Sam Gilbert, whom he called "UCLA's biggest booster." There was also a trip to the South Bend Farmer's Market with his parents to deliver a few tickets for the game. It was as if ticket requests outnumbered the arena seats by a three-to-one margin. Finally, there was lunch with his wife and the staff's California connection, Julian Labosky, a friend who often videotaped West Coast games and then mailed them to the Irish coaches. Basically it was just bumping into one friend after another for Digger. Even a friend of his from Rider College, Tom Petroff, showed up for the day. Eventually Digger and Danny Nee sneaked off to a racquetball court to get in an hour's workout. Everything was set and the coaches needed a distraction of their own as they waited for the team mass, meal, and then finally, the game.

There were five basic elements that Digger felt would insure a win against the Bruins as he briefed the team that night, December 11. The first was attacking UCLA's pressure defense with dribbling, poise, and patience. Larry Brown had his charges playing aggressive defense with zone and half-court trap presses. If Notre Dame guards and forwards did not pick up their dribble, Bruin defenders could tie them up and force bad passes. Digger wanted his kids to break the press by dribbling and then taking the ball to the hoop to score. He was hoping for a basket before the Bruin defense was set, striking quickly before the team could recover from the full- or half-court pressure.

Offensive rebounding was another area of concern, but this goal of "fierceness on the offensive boards" was nothing new. Digger had stressed this with his front-line players all along, reminding them to be court conscious, maintain floor balance, and spread out so that they'd be distributed around the basket if UCLA missed a rebounding opportunity.

The third factor was pure execution of all offenses, again stressing patience and working for the high-percentage shot. Digger forewarned the players they must make at least 80 percent of their foul shots: "Just grab for the rim, shoot with your system, and make sure you get your body going through the same motion."

The fifth item was probably the crucial one. Phelps left it for last so it would stay with the team as they warmed up. "To win it's going to take post defense, pressure defense, and defensive rebounding," he emphasized. This game would be the test: could the team execute its multiple defensive system without its main cog, Billy Hanzlik?

"It's been ten months since they beat you here," said Digger in his final pitch to the team. "If you're patient, you've got forty minutes to win this thing. The crowd wants it, you want it, and you've worked hard to get here. If you have the same emotion as they do, you'll win it because you're a better team than UCLA. Let's blow the roof off and win it."

As Digger took the floor the capacity crowd was taken back by the unusual attire of the fashionable coach. He breezed onto the court in yellow doubleknit practice slacks and a blue and gold Notre Dame jersey that football coach Ara Parseghian had made fashionable during his reign as the central figure on the Irish sports scene. During the summer Digger had heard that Brown was planning on buying a $400 suit to outdress him on his home court, so now he wore the football jersey to "get in Larry Brown's mind before the game." By fashion standards Larry was the best dressed, but on the Notre Dame campus the Parseghian style was still in vogue. Now it was Digger's turn to don the blue and gold jersey.

The crowd was on its feet, screaming and applauding as Digger went through his antics of gesturing for more applause and pretending not to hear the din. He worked his way to center court, exactly the way he wanted it, but seeming a bit uncomfortable as he scanned the student body. He was motioning to the stands inexplicably—until all at once his motive became clear. Suddenly Billy Hanzlik and Rich Branning were seen coming down the aisles of the student section with the other team members divided behind them. It was another gimmick; the students erupted with an even louder roar of applause as the team streamed through their ranks. UCLA had always been billed as the students' game and Digger once again had dreamed up a way to draw them into the contest even more.

Forward Tracy Jackson didn't take long to hit a ten-foot jump shot, putting the visiting Bruins at a disadvantage. That deficit didn't last long, however, and after leading by four points, Notre Dame squandered the lead by allowing Wilkes and Gig Sims two offensive rebound scores. When Wilkes tied the game with 9:55 left in the half Digger quickly jumped up from his familiar squat and signaled for a time out by jamming his fingers into the palm of his other hand. One would have thought all four digits would swell up from the jamming as Digger scowled at his team.

"You're too anxious. Everyone is trying to do it by himself and we're breaking down," he shouted above the crowd. "That's what happened last year—we tried to stick them by twenty and we ended up not scoring ourselves. You can beat them; take it two-by-two-by-two. You're trying to blow them out, but you can't do it yet. Now do it my way."

Digger now substituted with Mike Mitchell, Gil Salinas, and Tim Andree going in after the time out. Still, nothing seemed to go right. The team appeared to have ignored the key points the coaching staff had calculated would win the game. Turnovers, hurried shots, and lackluster rebounding characterized the home team's play through twenty minutes. At times Digger was graphic as he attempted to wake the players from their doldrums. The Irish entered the locker room trailing by six points, 36–30. Digger had words to match the situation.

"There wasn't one guy out there, with the possible exception of Stan Wilcox, who played consistent defense," he told the team. He pointed out missed assignments, poor shot selection, and inconsistencies as if he were a play-by-play commentator. "You're playing just like you did last year; you've played three straight halves against UCLA where you're not responding. They're running their fast break, hitting offensive rebounds, and we're thirteen for thirty from the field with fifteen turnovers." If he could have looked further at the statistics he would have seen that his starters had accounted for thirteen of the turnovers.

As the players took a drink or washed up, Digger huddled with his assistants and looked over the Bruins' first-half offenses in a diagrammed fashion. After outlining some adjustments on the chalkboard it was time to instill the team with the confidence they had lacked in the first half.

Digger outlined the game plan again, telling the players to go back to their mental edge. His manner was quiet as he led into his closing remarks. "We're trailing by six points—not twelve, but six. They're looking for a spurt, but damn it all, we have to play as a team, not individuals." He was shouting now. "You're not playing St. Louis or Northwestern. You're playing a team that's kicking the crap out of you and they're doing it in every phase of the game.

"What's your excuse? Play hard because UCLA walked in here laughing at you and they're still laughing. What are you made of; are you that soft? Get tough, play your asses off. Don't you let the students down."

Now his tone softened. "Gil, you did a good job; so did you, Mike. Be ready. We have to contribute through our roles and now is the time. Confidence is where it's at now; we believe in you, the students believe in you, and now it's time for you to start believing in yourself. Do it your way as a team."

The Irish continued their blundering until five minutes were left. UCLA freshman Rod Foster utilized his speed, hitting eleven points. The Bruins went up by nine points as Foster dished off to Sanders for an easy layup. As the game entered the final minutes the attention shifted to the free-throw line. Sims missed the first half of a bonus situation with UCLA leading, 71–66. Two seconds ticked away and Tripucka stepped to the charity stripe himself, making two shots to start an Irish surge. Foster added a jumper, and then Tyren Naulls hit one of two foul shots to restore UCLA's margin to 74–68 with 2:12 left in the game.

It was the final Bruin score. Center Orlando Woolridge now hit a midrange jumper to bring the Irish within four and then Tripucka made two more free throws to narrow the lead to two points. Tracy Jackson stepped to the line and made one of two to make the score 74–73 UCLA with only thirty-five seconds left. Notre Dame needed the ball and Darren Daye was fouled to stop the clock with just fifteen ticks remaining. Daye missed and with five seconds left the freshman, John Paxson, took a jumper from eighteen feet as the A.C.C. crowd held its breath. He missed, but he was fouled. It was time to evaluate the Irish recruiting efforts.

The year before it had been a UCLA freshman who made the last four points of the game to beat the Irish. Paxson stepped calmly to the line, sinking both free throws to put Notre Dame ahead for the first time in almost thirty minutes. To top it off, Paxson stole the inbounds pass and was intentionally fouled by Naulls. Pandemonium broke out as the celebration began.

Kelly Tripucka had been at the other end of the court when he began to dash toward Paxson to congratulate him. Somehow in the scramble, Kelly ran into the outstretched elbow of an official, jarring a tooth loose as blood spewed from his mouth. In the confusion someone on the bench remarked that a UCLA player had elbowed Kelly; the words set Digger off as he rushed to get to his own fallen player. As he approached Tripucka, Larry Brown tried to speak to him. Digger overreacted. Thinking a UCLA player had hit Kelly, he said, "Larry, I don't need this kind of stuff." Brown tried to object, but Digger repeated his feelings. A bad situation became worse. Even as Kelly was helped off the court, Digger still did not know he had been misinformed. Paxson finally made both free throws and the Irish won, 77–74. But the moment of victory was quickly diminished by the injury and the incidents of the closing two seconds.

In the locker room, while Tripucka quietly sobbed in obvious pain, Digger told the team they had played well. UCLA had outscored the Irish 66–54 from the floor, but Notre Dame had capitalized from the free-throw line, going twenty-three for twenty-eight to the Bruins, dismal eight-for-nineteen performance. "You didn't let up and you stole a game," Digger said. "It's a sign of a great team to be able to steal a big game. That's what it takes to win at Lexington and Market Square Arena. We made mistakes, but we bounced back. Tomorrow we're off and Thursday [Dec. 13] we play St. Joseph. The next most important thing you face is your final exams. If you're getting a B-minus now I want a solid B. Push yourselves."

As the players bowed their heads, Digger asked them to pray for Kelly's quick recovery—and to realize their potential. He dismissed them by telling them to party that night because they had earned it.

Before he could enjoy his own celebration he had to face the press in a postgame conference. "UCLA did a lot of good things to prevent us from playing according to our game plan," he said. "Larry Brown has done a great job and they're an ever-improving team that will have to be reckoned with by the end of the season." He also detailed Tripucka's injury situation and the confusion that followed. A Chicago *Sun-Times* writer grilled him on the student body's conduct during the game when a roll of toilet paper was tossed at the Bruin bench: "Do you think the crowd's behavior was a little beyond the limits of acceptability?" Digger admitted that it was wrong but added that Notre Dame ran into it on the road, too, especially in West Virginia. That wasn't enough for the writer who was pressing for a story other than the Irish victory. "Maybe by not coming out before the game and inflaming the crowd, it could have been prevented," he suggested. Digger would have none of that.

"That's just me; I'm a cheerleader coach. This goes on all over the country. We played at North Carolina State last year and there were some signs I wouldn't want my mother to see. If that's what you saw in the ball game, fine. It will happen at Pauley and everywhere else when students are in that position. I guess the only thing left is to take the toilet paper out of the dorms. Does anyone want to talk about the game now?"

Later, Notre Dame officials, sportswriters, coaches, and wives gathered for a party at Digger's house. Father Joyce, the university's vice-president, stopped by to congratulate the coach and his staff. *Sports Illustrated's* Larry Keith and Curry Fitzpatrick were also in attendance with Digger's good friend, Dave Israel of the Chicago *Tribune*. Digger was drained as he mingled with his guests, savoring the victory but declining to relive it. It was time to relax. His efforts over the past year had passed his semiannual measuring-stick test.

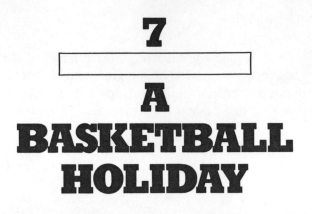

7

A BASKETBALL HOLIDAY

The Pumas of St. Joseph's College in Rensselaer, Indiana, had the perfect chance to beat Notre Dame—if they could in fact bring it off. St. Joseph's was a tiny Division II team that did not look like much on paper, having lost five senior lettermen to graduation. If the Irish were going to be upset before they played Kentucky at the end of the month, this would be the game to do it. The players might still be thinking about the UCLA victory, beating the Bruins in a thriller before the home fans. Digger would also be without regulars Tripucka and Branning, relegated to the bench with injuries. If the Pumas were ever going to catch Notre Dame sleeping and register their first victory ever against the Irish, tonight's game might witness the upset.

Digger prepared his charges by showing them films of the UCLA game and pointing out the glaring mistakes that had been so obvious to him from his spot in front of the Irish bench. He hoped that would bring his club back to reality. "There were a lot of things you didn't do defensively against UCLA," he said. "I think the films bore this out. By evaluating your efforts against a good team you know what you need to get it done, so that we don't slip along the way."

Digger's manner had changed noticeably since the UCLA game. (He had called Larry Brown to apologize for overreacting and Larry had said all was forgiven.) What a difference two nights could make. He was calm, relaxed, addressing the team as if he were a grandfather. "We've got to take advantage of a win, taking the negatives and turning those into positives so that we improve as a team," he said quietly. Without Branning and Tripucka the starting roles would go to Salinas and Mitchell—the first starting assignments of their careers. "This is where we need you guys: it's your turn to be designated hitters. Get out there and take your swings."

To win against the Pumas, he told his club to control the tempo and get into a running game, to exploit St. Joseph's bench weakness. It was obvious that the opposition talent could not stack up to Notre Dame's. Solid team defense, offensive execution, and rebounding were the three goals for the night. Especially defense.

"Tonight's the night to work on a particular weakness," Digger stressed. "If you give up the baseline on a drive, try to work on that shortcoming. Do one thing, work on one weakness on defense, and we'll get what we want out of this game."

Digger had hoped the game would be over in seven minutes as the team broke from the huddle to take the floor. It almost came true as the Irish jumped out to a 19–9 lead against the outclassed Pumas. Guard Mike Mitchell made the most of his starting role, hitting the first basket of the night and scoring ten points before the half. Mike had undergone microdot surgery in September. After the team's first meeting, he was playing basketball at the Rockne Memorial, a campus gym noted for some pretty tough student pickup games. The sophomore from California tried to cut when his left knee gave out, tearing cartilage and ligaments. On September 17, Dr. Lanny Johnson of East Lansing, Michigan, operated on Mitchell through three tiny puncture wounds in his knee; the method was gaining popularity throughout the United States. There was no scar to heal; it was just a matter of regaining the strength in the knee. With the support of trainer Skip Meyer, Mitchell went through a rigorous recovery program that included a daily swim and progressive resistance exercises. He had covered quite a bit of ground to prepare for his starting role, and did not want to strike out as a "designated hitter." Nor did he. By halftime the Irish led 50–23. It was time to throw in the towel, but Puma coach George Waggoner did not want to stop the fight. There was still one round left.

At the half Digger did quite a bit of diagramming, pointing out plays as if he were a professor writing class notes on the board. It was a good opportunity to work with a different unit, to talk about game situations some of the players hadn't yet experienced. Digger praised his makeshift lineup, offering only one criticism and that in mild tones: "On the foul line, going eight for seventeen is embarrassing." The concentration on the line wasn't there, an unacceptable condition even with a twenty-seven–point lead.

There were some signs of a lackadaisical attitude in the second half as the Pumas outscored the Irish, 35–29. Digger scolded the team, but the players were still good enough to win, 79–58. Mitchell finished the game with fourteen points, the same total he had contributed in the previous year's NCAA first-round game—in a similar subbing role. Woolridge also set an A.C.C. shooting record, going seven for seven from the floor. Now, the only thing Digger wanted was thirteen eligible players after final exams.

Digger gave the team three days off, asking them to come in for a brief one-hour workout on Monday to run some drills. The break in the final-exam routine should be refreshing, he said. Nervous energy always abounded in the dorms during the semester exam period. "If you can, run in the building or outside if the weather is nice. I think it will help you study. You'll be able to sleep better, get your rest, and still stay in shape for us." After exams the team would practice Thursday and Friday, then play Fairfield on Saturday, three days before Christmas.

"That leads up to the next event, Christmas night, when we practice next," said Digger. He was organizing the team grab-bag for the Christmas-night party at his house. It was a good thing he and Nee were better organized at planning a game. They certainly had a tough time organizing the team for the party.

Digger passed the hat over each player's head, explaining how to select a name. "Now when you get your little name out of the hat you hide it," he instructed, in a whining tone that he often used to fool his youngest daughter, Jennifer. "You don't say 'I got na-na-na-na.'" The players broke up around him. "It's a surprise. Do we understand the drill?" he asked, telling everyone the limit was five dollars. Tripucka picked first, but Hanzlik piped up that if he picked Tracy's name he was buying bananas to go with Jackson's "Magilla Gorilla" nickname. The team had loosened up and so had its coaches. Orlando was trying to look into the hat before he picked, but Digger told him not to peek. "It's not Biology or Economics," he scoffed. The coaches and managers were also included in the draw, along with Skip Meyer. After the draw it was time for a quick prayer for the sick, the hostages in Iran—and for the team to get through final exams. Someone must have been listening to the last request.

When Barry Spencer was playing at Garfinkel's Five-Star Basketball Camp between his high school sophomore and junior years, he was one of the camp's best players. That was in some pretty fast company, including John Paxson and other high schoolers a year older. But before Spencer could get through the first few games of his junior year, he broke his ankle and sat out the entire year. For the first few games of his senior year, he was getting back into his game.

Digger and Danny Nee flew out of South Bend in the early evening on Pete Pilliod's plane. The Irish had just finished a lengthy practice five days before Christmas. Nee had talked Digger into coming to see Spencer in Columbus, Ohio. Thanks to Pete's prop jet, the pair were able to get to Columbus in less than an hour, lopping off four hours of travel time the trip would have taken if they drove.

While in flight, the Irish coaches reflected on a scrimmage that the second team had won at the buzzer on a shot by Hanzlik. In some ways, the second string seemed hungrier and more willing to take instructions. The coaches realized that was a luxury they'd need before the year was out. Danny, Tommy, and Scotty had refereed the scrimmage, letting many fouls go uncalled to prepare the team for the rough game expected against Kentucky in Freedom Hall. At one point, Tripucka had complained about being fouled in the act of shooting, but Nee replied that his whistle wouldn't blow until Kelly started playing some tough defense.

The recruiting duo found the Columbus Fairgrounds, thanks to a few good guesses when it came time to turn. Digger had been at the fairgrounds a year earlier, when he was recruiting Paxson. Chomping a few hot dogs and downing some coffee, Digger, Danny, and Pete headed for a deserted corner of the arena where they could watch Spencer against a local Ohio team. Spencer was less than spectacular, but this wasn't too disturbing to Digger. Often, the sight of a head coach makes a prospective player tighten up and stray from his normal game. That night Barry started the game out cold, missing a few shots that washed away his confidence. The heralded high school All-America did finish with thirteen points, but it was nowhere near his normal effort, as he never got into the flow of the game. During the game, Detroit Central Catholic's coach prodded Barry to "do something because Digger's here." The Irish were definite favorites with the coach, but Digger worried that the added influence might hurt Notre Dame's chances of signing Spencer.

"Barry did some things tonight that I liked. He handled the ball well, he's physical, and he's an athlete," said Digger after the game. He had seen a player go through a bad night before; Tim Andree always froze up when Digger and Danny visited him as a high school senior. It was something to be expected. "When his offensive game fell apart, he let it affect the rest of his game, too," Digger added. "He just has to build his confidence to a point where that doesn't bother him." Spencer was visibly down, but the Irish coaches encouraged him to put it out of his mind: Notre Dame was still interested in him as a player and a student. Spencer had the numbers in class, too. Notre Dame had recruited him academ- ically—even before the basketball coaches became interested— because of his 3.7 grade-point average. The problem was that Notre Dame wasn't the only school in the picture. A Duke assistant coach was also at the game, along with Ohio State Coach Eldon Miller. Still, Notre Dame appeared to be the best choice for Barry, because of his desire to become an architect. Duke coaches were encouraging him to enroll as an engineering student instead. Digger felt confident that if the decision was a family one, Barry would choose Notre Dame. If not, his chances dropped to fifty-fifty. The pair headed back to South Bend feeling good about the trip, hoping that Barry would fulfill their need for a perimeter shooter. The low-key recruiting approach would have to continue for a while longer while Barry made up his mind himself.

There were three distractions the Irish had to overcome when they hosted Fairfield University. Nine days of final exams, an impending Christmas holiday, and an unranked opponent were hurdles Digger shared with the team in a pregame pep talk. Before their visit to the Athletic and Convocation Center, Fairfield was playing under the five hundred mark. All the elements were present for an upset and Digger wanted to prepare his players mentally and physically. In the back of his mind, he felt that the rigorous final-exam schedule would hurt his team's momentum. So he went the psychological route. Concentration and execution were the key words he posted in the players' lockers. If they concentrated on the floor that day, the alertness might make up for any weariness or rough edges.

At the outset of the game it looked as if Digger's ploy had worked. Notre Dame broke quickly from the gate, building a 26–10 lead before the Irish coach went to his bench to relieve the front line. But as Digger substituted, the Stags got back into the game. At the half Notre Dame was leading by ten points, but that margin diminished in the second twenty minutes. Twice Fairfield cut Notre Dame's lead to five points by spreading out the Irish defense and setting up some back-door baskets. By playing a control game, coach Fred Barakat calculated that the Irish defense wouldn't be as effective helping each other out. The strategy worked. Layups were the order of the night as the visitors shot 66 percent from the field. Poise paid off for Notre Dame, though, as they won, 76–66.

"They spread us out, keeping the ball in the middle and having everyone try to backdoor against our front line," Digger admitted. "It was a good strategy; it kept them close and they left South Bend with a respectable score." Before the contest Irish fans had been talking of a forty-point victory margin. But under such circumstances Digger would never have resorted to running it up—unless, perhaps, he was repaying his opposing bench director for past history.

Toward the end of the game, the Irish ran through some of the zone defenses they would be employing against Kentucky. Billy Hanzlik also logged some playing time for the first time since the Russian game. "Billy wasn't that sharp tonight," said Digger, "but he needs court time to get ready for Kentucky on December 29. It's a sacrifice you make tonight to prepare for the rest of the schedule."

Kentucky, San Francisco, and Tulane loomed on the Irish schedule and this was on Digger's mind. The Irish defensive effort that he builds his teams on hadn't been as evident as he would have liked it to be. With Orlando in the middle and small forwards Jackson and Tripucka on the flanks, the front line's defense and rebounding had suffered. Digger contemplated the possibility of playing Andree more in the slot, a position at which the freshman felt more comfortable than Woolridge, a true forward. Keeping

Tripucka and Jackson off the court at the same time—even whole-sale changes in the starting lineup—might also be a solution. Whatever the answer, Digger was already thinking of shaking up the team before Christmas to get the most out of his players.

In reality, the holiday season was the last thing on the coach's mnd as the team took the next few days for a short vacation with their families. The Christmas spirit didn't come easily for Digger. It wasn't that he wanted to play Scrooge or that the holidays didn't stir his personal religious feelings. It was the image of the Kentucky Wildcats waiting to ambush the Irish at Freedom Hall that domi-nated his thoughts. Digger's teams had lost five straight games to the Wildcats since a 94–79 win in the 1973–74 season. Before that there had been two additional losses while Digger was beginning his reign as Irish coach. The only thing he really wanted for Christmas was a box containing a winning game plan for the Kentucky contest. He didn't mind if it was labeled "Do Not Open until December 29."

In the meantime there were holiday routines that Digger couldn't neglect as a husband, father, or coach. One day there was the A.C.C. Christmas party for all the building's maintenance workers. For weeks Digger had clowned with the staff, warning them the skits had better be good this year. It meant rescheduling a recruiting trip, but it was one of those holiday rituals he had to attend. It was also one of the few times he could escape from coaching for an hour or two.

There was also time out for the family as the Wildcats approached. Digger and his kids selected a giant blue spruce for the living room and there was also the beef Wellington Christmas dinner Terry cooked for the family. For three days Phelps forced himself to forget about coaching and the Kentucky game. Even then, the escape wasn't easy.

"I shouldn't have to force myself to enjoy one of the great moments of the year," he remarked to a reporter. "Everyone, Christians and non-Christians, looks forward to Christmas. One day a year to be at peace. I guess many people have their problems invade their thoughts the way the Kentucky game pervades mine." He mentioned a friend of his battling cancer, the hostages in Iran. "There's no way my problems compare with those crises; I guess I'm fortunate the Kentucky game is meaningless in the scheme of things."

Digger doesn't like being more wrapped up in college basketball than in Christmas. He often wonders aloud what it would be like if he were able to go through a Christmas week without worrying about a basketball game—enjoying the quiet times with his wife and kids and not being preoccupied with scouting reports, films, practices, and game plans. And also, of course, recruiting, a coaching chore that never ceases. These are the disadvantages that accompany a college coaching job, responsibilities that can't be shirked if a winning tradition is to continue. But there are other aspects of the job that specially appeal to Digger.

At thirty-eight, he is looked on as one of the country's top college basketball coaches. After starting as a junior-high coach he had a rapid rise. Like all successful people he also has an ego. He can step out of it for the good of his family or team, but he relishes the glamour of the Notre Dame position. If he was out of coaching, he'd be on edge until he got back in. The lifestyle suits his personality.

"I know I'm demanding with my assistants and my family," he told the reporter. "But I don't put any more demands on them than I put on myself." He recalled something Terry—a language-doctorate student—told him as she took off for a Modern Language Association meeting in San Francisco: "She warned me not to overreact to Kentucky." Terry meant don't be too hard on the kids, the assistants, or yourself, Digger admitted. And then, without realizing it, he lapsed into the pregame thinking he and his coaches had been going over during their preparation for the Wildcats. "Sure I want to beat them, and if we handle it mentally, keep them off the boards, and react to Kyle Macy, we'll win." That desire to win burned a hole through every other topic.

The pressure built up. Digger even went a little crazy Christmas night. It was an escapade that started at his home and ended in football coach George Kelly's bedroom. The beginning was innocent enough: a team Christmas party at Digger's, where the coaches, players, trainer, and manager exchanged gifts. Most of the gifts were gag jokes, aimed good-naturedly at some player's quirk. Tracy Jackson, who somehow earned the nickname Magilla, got several small Magilla Gorilla toys. There was also a Mr. Potato Head for Billy Hanzlik—something about resemblance somewhere. And there was Digger, dressed up like Santa Claus with a set of glasses and false nose. After the party broke up, Santa made a visit to Sports Information Director Roger Valdiserri's house, peeking in the window until someone noticed the strange face. It didn't stop there; Santa made his final call at George Kelly's, walking by George's wife and jumping into bed with the Irish linebacker coach. When George woke up and found a strange bedmate, he didn't immediately realize who it was. Then, as Kelly went downstairs in a robe and slippers, ready for a nightcap, Digger stole out as a good Santa would.

"I guess I needed to go crazy," said Digger the next morning.

8

BLUE GRASS BLUES

The Kentucky series has meant nothing but frustration for Digger and his Irish team. Notre Dame lost to the Wildcats at Louisville's Freedom Hall in Digger's first year, and there has only been one win—during the 1973–74 season—since then. There have been humbling moments for Digger over the years, even when he has been happy about his team's efforts. In his rookie year, his makeshift squad lost 83–67 to the immortal Adolph Rupp. That defeat had been almost easy to swallow after the two sound drubbings that preceded the Wildcat game. Indiana had annihilated Notre Dame by sixty-five points, 94–29, and then the UCLA Bruins had picked up where the Hoosiers left off with a 114–56 victory. Surprisingly, the Irish were within sixteen points of Rupp's charges and Digger looked at the Kentucky game as an improvement—until he received a phone call back at his hotel. It was Adolph Rupp and Digger expected some encouraging words for the struggling upstart. Instead, he was floored.

"Rupp was at a victory party and he said there was something he couldn't figure out," Digger recalls with a smile. "He said, 'You've lost to Bobby Knight by sixty-five and John Wooden by fifty-eight points, so how come we were able to beat you by only sixteen points.' Rupp worried about his club."

Since that christening, Digger's frustration has continued, with losses by as little as two points just a year later and as many as two dozen points. Year after year the Irish traveled south after Christmas to play Kentucky at Louisville's Freedom Hall before at least 16,000 fans. Years before, there had been an incident at Notre Dame's Field House, where the spectators were especially hard on the visitors. Kentucky officials did not want to return there, so the series was kept alive by playing at a "neutral site." Through an oversight along the way, Notre Dame entered into a long-term contract that named Freedom Hall as the "neutral site." It was a cross Phelps inherited and a situation that helped create a myth that Notre Dame couldn't win at Freedom Hall. Digger couldn't wait to get Kentucky in South Bend for a game, but first he'd have to live with those 16,613 noisy "neutral" fans in Louisville.

For two weeks he had plotted a strategy, pointing to the game as a national championship contest that would be the third step in his team development. The Russians were the first step and the UCLA game was a shaky second step in the right direction. Now it was time to face a powerhouse on the road, a chance to develop the character so necessary to carry a team to the NCAA finals. Digger had been so intense about beating the Wildcats that every conversation somehow got around to the Kentucky game. "I'm just sick of losing to Kentucky. This game is like a football team's bowl game," he once told sportswriters. "We've had time to prepare for just one team, not two or three that we might face a week later in the season." Digger well remembered the Sugar Bowl Game, where Ara Parseghian's team beat Alabama, 24–23, for the national title. He recalled the hostile Crimson Tide fans the Irish gridders had encountered and compared them to the Kentucky "blue wave" that would fill the Freedom Hall. There were no studies, no exams, nothing to distract his players. Digger could concentrate on basketball, and he capitalized on the opportunity.

The players probably would have known it was a big game even if Digger hadn't taken a more active role in practice, pointing out situations personally, and not leaving much to his coaches. "If the kids see me running through plays with them, pointing out this or yelling about that, it will shake them up," he said. "They've got to realize—even more than they do already—that this is an important game if I get so involved with all the scouting and practice workouts."

There were other signs that the Wildcat contest was very important in the season scheme Digger had devised. The pocket-size game card was filled with condensed strategy. Digger had outlined important plays with colored pens, as one of his players might highlight a novel or textbook preparing for an exam. There were different colors for offenses, defenses, and time-out plans.

Digger color-codes the games he feels are the most important and this turned out to be the first rainbow-hued game card of the year.

On the morning of the Kentucky game, Digger usually allows the players some time to loosen up at Freedom Hall. It gives the team a chance to get a feel for the rims and backboard, and to start becoming accustomed to the hostile surroundings. Part of that adjustment procedure includes a thorough heckling by Kentucky fans, who rise early on Saturday to give the Notre Dame players a good going over as they practice some foul-shooting or work on their outside game. This Saturday Digger decided against the negative atmosphere and instead took the team on a tour of Churchill Downs Racetrack. It was a good distraction for the team, and Digger thought it might ease the tension a little. There would be enough time for jeering that night.

If Digger were to beat the Wildcats, it would be a tainted success in the mind of Kentucky fans and the press. Guard Dwight Anderson had left the team and the university, one of fifteen players since 1972 who had started their college career at Kentucky and then chose to finish it at another institution. Two other players, freshman center Sam Bowie and classmate Dirk Minniefield, had been suspended for the Notre Dame contest by Coach Joe B. Hall. The crutch was there: if the Irish won, it would be because of the absence of Bowie, Minniefield, and Anderson. If the Wildcats still managed to win, it would just enhance the mystique of Kentucky's dominance of the Irish at their favorite "neutral site."

"I want you to be conditioned to play big games on the road, before hostile fans, with adversity or team problems," Digger told a quiet locker room a half-hour before the tip-off. "Kentucky has a team problem now, but let's not kid ourselves. They're playing it up as a team problem; but Bowie, Anderson, and Minniefield were not factors in their wins." He cited the Wildcats' win against Indiana when the three players weren't in the game, and then against Purdue where their presence wasn't felt either. "They've beaten Indiana and Purdue," he said; "now they want to own the entire state of Indiana."

After having spent hours watching films and videotapes of Kentucky games, Digger now urged his club to play its own game. He warned that Kentucky would come out aggressively, playing as if in a national championship game. "They always play that way," he added, "and why not? Kentucky won't quit—they'll come back with two minutes left."

Digger wanted the team to warm up at the far basket, so that he could direct the defense in the second half. "We're going to win this game with defense in that second half," he predicted. "The way I see it, you're already down nine points when the official throws the ball in the air for the tip-off. Don't play scared, play hard and aggressive. Kentucky teams play with a fire inside them and you also have to have that fire." No one could deny that Digger had fire as he rattled off characteristics the Wildcats had exhibited in jumping out to a 10–1 season mark. They'd charged out of the starting gate and they wouldn't quit.

The team was silent as Digger drew analogies between the Pittsburgh Pirates' family atmosphere and the fact that the Bucs won the last two games of the World Series on the road at Baltimore. He hoped his family model would inspire communication, poise, and confidence. "This is one of those moments we live for in sports," he said. "This is also our first important game on the road." Digger went on. "It's just like Pauley Pavilion. You can win there and you can win at Freedom Hall. Go after them—if they knock you down you knock them down. Don't fight, but play hard."

Digger also appealed to the team's pride. "People don't think you're that good; the country doesn't think you're that good. That's just the politics of the conference schools against you, a rap that we don't have what it takes to win a national championship. Let's show the nation what we've been working on since last March when Michigan State beat us at Market Square. It's a mental game and you're mental giants. Now let's go show the nation just what we have."

Digger and the coaches thought they had the game plan to beat the Wildcats. Starting with a man-to-man full-court press, Digger hoped to take away the driving lanes and begin aggressively. That aggressive intensity headed the key points on the blackboard entitled "To Win Against Kentucky." Taking the ball to score was another concept he stressed, relying on second efforts with no excuses for mistakes. The coaches also hoped that poise, patience, and confidence on offense would help the team overcome the surroundings. Making over 80 percent of the foul shots summed up the master plan. For the team it would be a battle against Kentucky; for Digger, a crusade.

As it turned out Digger was right about the Wildcats' propensity for exploding at once. With the guiding hands of senior floor general Kyle Macy, Kentucky surged ahead 14–6 in the first six minutes. The senior All-America hit three jump shots and junior forward Fred Cowan scored three straight baskets, better than half of his nine-point-a-game season average. Cowan and Macy surely didn't realize their team was weakened by the loss of Anderson, Minniefield, and Bowie.

The Wildcats took advantage of poor defensive execution by the Irish, finding it easy to break Notre Dame's press defense and scoring fourteen layups in the first twenty minutes against some ineffective front-line defense. The statistics at the half told the entire story. Kentucky was beating the Irish on the boards 20–15, and controlling rebounds well enough to make twenty-two of thirty-five field goals for a 63-percent mark. Notre Dame on the other hand was scratching its way through a shooting drought, converting thirty-two shots into an anemic total of eleven baskets. It would take more than a 34-percent shooting performance to beat Kentucky in Freedom Hall—a fact Digger reminded his team of in intermission. Still, Notre Dame could come back from a 47–33 deficit with strong play in the final half.

Digger encouraged his team to respond better on defense, to be patient for the good shots, and to control the offensive and defensive boards. It was too late.

The second half started better, but Kentucky was able to match the Irish intensity with their patented "fire." With five minutes gone Kentucky's margin slipped to ten points and then grew to fourteen. Notre Dame slimmed the lead to ten points when Joe B. was slapped with a technical, and then cut it further to 69–63 with eight minutes left. Notre Dame struggled to dent the Kentucky advantage, but never pulled closer than six points. Macy hit a key three-point play down the stretch and Kentucky made the free throws when it counted in the closing moments. Despite some last minute heroics by Branning, Wilcox, Woolridge, and Varner, the difference never diminished beyond a six-point Kentucky margin. The Irish lost 86–80. It was a disappointing effort.

The sullen Notre Dame locker room was quiet except for the Kentucky fans celebrating outside in the arena. Joe B. Hall left the court on the shoulders of his players. Digger left with the task of pulling his players together.

"You made a run at it and didn't quit," he said. "I'm proud of you for that." But he was visibly disappointed, exhaling in disgust as he added, "Yes, it stinks. Nobody likes a defeat."

He also lost no time in starting to plan ahead: "We've got to regroup and get some things straight mentally. You didn't quit, but we didn't hit the foul shots and play the defense we needed. You'll see them again in March, but there are two tough road games you have to start thinking about right now—San Francisco and Tulane." Tulane had already played Louisiana State and lost by a mere point, a fact Digger hoped would keep his team from taking them too lightly. He wound up by falling back on his family concept: "Let's mature from this experience and go have a team meal at Dominick Mattai's. We need to get our heads together as a unit." Relatives and friends were welcome at the annual eating extravaganza. A win would have made it so much tastier, though.

Before the dinner Digger had to face the Kentucky press. "I've been coming down here nine years now and I'm one and eight," he admitted. "I have a humbling experience every New Year's." Digger said the things the press wanted to hear, and his praise of Macy and the Wildcats made their way into the quotes page compiled and distributed by the Kentucky Sports Information Department. His debate with one sportswriter about the importance of the missing trio did not.

Digger was attempting to explain the roles of Joe B. Hall's missing-in-action contingent, but the writer wouldn't have any part of it, so Digger finally reversed the situation, asking him about the Purdue and Indiana games. He said "Read the stats. You'll find what you're looking for. You saw *THE* Kentucky team here tonight. *THE* Kentucky team." Another reporter prefaced a question by saying that Kentucky played a tougher schedule than Digger's Irish, but Digger summed things up by comparing it to any other game at Freedom Hall in the last nine years.

Joe B. Hall saw the game differently, noting that his club was within one basket of "blowing it out." As for his technical foul, Hall remarked that he didn't understand it. "I felt very upset over the technical because I stood there while Digger Phelps lectured for a solid minute and he [the official] took it like a gentleman," said Hall. "I stood up and asked him one question and got a technical. I don't like that. I don't understand that."

9

IRISH
HOMECOMINGS

Notre Dame's schedule is as national as its recruiting, and, in fact, the two go hand in hand. When Digger Phelps and his staff recruit a player, there's usually a promise to that athlete and his family that at least once in his career he'll play a game against a team close to his home town. It's an unusual promise for a head coach to make to a high school athlete, one that might be difficult to fulfill at a state university or conference school. But thanks to Notre Dame's national following, Digger can make the most of his team's independent status. He can schedule the University of Michigan in the Silverdome, Fordham in Madison Square Garden, or Viginia outside of Chicago in Rosemont's New Horizon. Notre Dame's next three games would prove that Digger's recruiting pitch was more than rhetoric; Mike Mitchell, Orlando Woolridge, and Gilbert Salinas were coming home.

The San Francisco game, January 8, was sophomore guard Mike Mitchell's chance to again display his shooting style to Bay area fans who had watched Mike play his high school ball at nearby Capuchino High School. San Francisco was a formidable opponent despite a certain indifference shown by the media. Coach Don Belluomini was finding new ways to win without All-America center Bill Cartwright, who was serving his apprenticeship with the NBA's New York Knicks. Texas was the only blemish on the Dons' schedule through the first ten games and Oakland's Coliseum throng of over 13,000 would make sure the Irish were aware of their opponent's prowess. Digger was aware of his team's deficiencies after the Kentucky loss and he was striving to get his team back on the winning track. The bitterness from the Kentucky defeat traveled with him and the team as they arrived on the West Coast. The city of San Francisco is a personal favorite of Digger's: he looked forward to the

RUSSIAN PREPARATIONS: Manager, Stacy Russo, and his trusty broom
helped Tracy Jackson get ready for the Russian's towering forms.
Tom Jackman—Notre Dame Observer

TIMEOUT TALK: If the team lacked "fire," Digger could always provide a little of his own brand *Brian Watkins*

AL McGUIRE ROAST: It was tough for the coaches to roast one of their own, but somehow they managed for charity! (*Left to Right:* Al McGuire, Digger, Ray Meyer) *Pat Scanlon*

ARMANDO'S BARBER SHOP: There's only one place to get your hair cut and catch up on the latest scuttlebutt: Armando's. *Pat Scanlon*

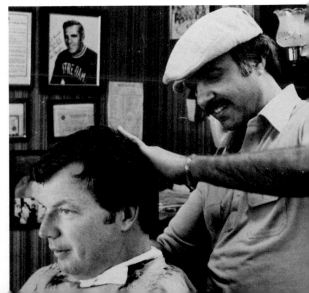

SIDELINES COACHING: A
stop in play is like time-out
in football; coaches should
use the pause to direct play.
Brother Charles McBride, C.S.C.

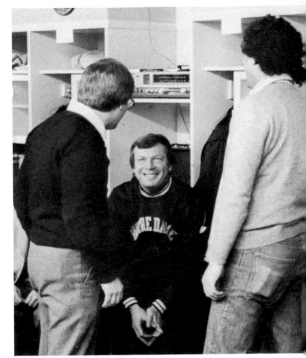

UCLA GAME #1: The cheerleader coach explains to *Sports Illustrated*'s Larry Keith (left), and Dave Israel of the *Chicago Tribune* (right), how he hoped to get into Larry Brown's mind before the UCLA game.
Pat Scanlon

PEP RALLY: Pep rallies were a Notre Dame football tradition that Digger wanted to carry over to basketball. *Pat Scanlon*

DIGGER'S SECRETARY, DOTTIE VAN PARIS: Dottie had the difficult chore of handling the tickets and the office work while sheltering her boss from the never-ending phone calls. *Pat Scanlon*

BENCH SHOT: Digger demanded concentration on the floor, the bench, and in the locker room
Brian Watkins

IRISH-MICHIGAN AT PONTIAC SILVERDOME: 38,000 fans watched the Irish and Michigan in 1979, the third largest crowd ever to watch a college basketball game. *Falc File Photos*

REFEREE BATTLE: "Don't worry about the referees, I'll handle them," noted Digger. *Falc File Photos*

BILL HANZLIK: Co-captain Bill Hanzlik's abilities were invaluable, his
worth became evident when he made the United States 1980 Olympic
team. *Brother Charles McBride, C.S.C.*

PLAYING TO CROWD: "What? Can't hear you," Phelps would say as he warmed up the crowd before a big game. *Falc File Photos*

UCLA GAME ENDING: For the fourth year in a row, a freshman decided the outcome. This time it was John Paxson's turn.
Brother Charles McBride, C.S.C.

LECTURING: Digger liked talking basketball, but not before putting it in perspective. *Pat Scanlon*

De PAUL GAME: UCLA, Marquette, San Francisco, and then De Paul all learned of the Irish giant killers.
Falc File Photos

THE ASSISTANTS: While the team gained its composure, the coaches would debate over a strategy. (*Left to Right:* Digger, Danny Nee, Tommy McLaughlin) *Brother Charles McBride, C.S.C.*

"DIGGER" PHELPS: Richard "Digger" Phelps and his co-author, Pat
Scanlon. *Pat Scanlon*

PETE PILLIOD PLANE SHOT: Digger disliked flying, but Pete Pilliod and
his pilot, Bill, made recruiting trips enjoyable. *Pat Scanlon*

FATHER THEODORE HESBURGH: "Father Hesburgh is a living saint,"
explained Digger after the San Francisco game.
Brother Charles McBride, C.S.C.

trip. He felt that the team would also enjoy the city—that it would give them a cultural experience along with the top-notch competitor the players would hopefully grow against. There were few doubts in Digger's mind that the Dons would be a difficult challenge for his team after the Kentucky loss and a ten day lay-off.

The night before the game the players went their separate ways sightseeing. Digger opted for a quiet dinner with his former assistant coaches, Dick DiBiaso and Dick Kuchen, joining Roger Valdiserri and Jim Gibbons, who were also members of the official party. "DeBo" was struggling a bit as coach of Stanford and "Kuch" was giving it his best at the University of California–Berkeley. The foursome ate Chinese food and enjoyed the leisurely atmosphere. But even over dinner, it was obvious that Digger was very involved in the upcoming game. He wanted to win badly.

Game day included some shopping. The clothes horse couldn't resist purchasing a multicolored sports coat at a bargain-basement price of $35. Digger claimed the jacket was worth $150, but there were some dissenting opinions on the value of the jacket. Digger didn't wear it for the game, but in retrospect it would have at least brightened up the gloomy performance of the Irish that night.

"This is a game where you just have to go out and be yourselves," Digger told the team in the bowels of the Oakland Coliseum Arena. He approached the contest as a chance to develop the mental phase of his club. It would mean putting the Wildcat defeat out of mind and possessing enough poise and confidence to beat a strong team on their home grounds. It was time to get back in the basketball groove, with the men in the roles that Digger counted on each of them to perform in his master plan.

It wasn't long into the contest before Digger and his staff realized the layoff between games had hurt the team. It was as if neither side wanted to win, both going sluggishly through the motions.

The final score was University of San Francisco 67, Notre Dame 59, but in the end the box score summed things up. The Irish were guilty of twenty-two turnovers and had suffered through a 39-percent shooting blight. If the team had executed its offensive patterns and controlled the game, as it could have, it would have been a more enjoyable flight to Shreveport, Louisiana. Instead the team was still looking for its first win of 1980 and attempting to break a losing streak that had mushroomed to two games. But it was not the end of the world for Digger, as his team would have a chance to redeem itself in two nights. Also, at the very least, Mike Mitchell had gotten his chance to play in front of his parents and home area fans. Digger had been true to his word.

And "reunion week" continued. As the Irish arrived at the Shreveport Airport, Orlando's parents and friends were there to welcome the team. It was an outgrowth of Digger's "family concept" for the season.

But this was not the only greeting. When Notre Dame loses two games in a row it's not unusual for the press to subject Digger's strategy to close scrutiny. Digger had already drawn the ire of a local newspaper columnist, who heavily quoted NBC commentator Billy Packer in a critical statement on Notre Dame's playing. The headline in the Birmingham *Post-Herald* read, "Basketball Analyst Mixes Humor with Biting Criticism." One thing for certain, Packer didn't spare many in his comments to sportswriter Paul Finebaum. Al McGuire, LSU Coach Dale Brown, Florida's John Lotz, and even NBC were all targets for the one-sided attack. (NBC drew Packer's wrath for its coverage of New Mexico's problems with gambling and transcript records. "I didn't think NBC did a very good job in exposing what happened there," Packer said.) As for John Lotz, the recently fired Florida coach, Packer ridiculed him—oddly enough—for being nothing more than an assistant coach for Dean Smith. On rebuilding the Florida program, Packer asked, "How is he going to be capable of it? How does he even walk into a high school kid's home and say 'Hi, I'm John Lotz from the University of Florida.' And the guy says 'Nice meeting you. I understand Joe Hall is coming in later.'"

The former Wake Forest assistant coach continued. "Lotz will start to say 'I'm losing it, I've lost my touch.' He never had it." And, according to Packer, "Dale Brown is the most misunderstood guy in coaching. The problem is nobody can quite understand him."

Even Al McGuire was brought into the article. Referring to a McGuire comment that a basketball player's socks are the driest article of clothing on a kid during a game, Packer said, "Al and I are close friends but some of that stuff he comes up with is unbelievable. There's no truth about the socks bit, but people at home will look at the screen and say 'That Al, he really knows what he's talking about.'"

By the time Packer got around to Digger, "the super pain" half of college basketball had been drawn into the commentary. Packer complained that Digger was always center stage. Last year we [NBC] had him on national television five times. He lost all five. He keeps giving me the A.C.C. this and the A.C.C. that. He plays Maryland, a sixth-place team, and loses....But Digger is in a world of his own. And hopefully with that schedule he'll win his twenty games, lose the five national television games, be rated in the Top Fifteen, and then get in the national playoff and get blown out by either the Big Ten or Southeastern Conference team."

Digger later talked with Billy, after declining to respond to the article in print. All he said was, "There's no reason to get drawn into that. Some people just don't understand what we have at Notre Dame and if they do they're just jealous." Packer explained that he was only having fun with the writer, that his comments were taken out of context. For Digger, the comments about Lotz couldn't be taken lightly. "I don't mind the comments about me. Billy's my friend and he might have been misquoted," Digger absolved. "It's the things he said about John Lotz that weren't funny, though. Sometimes Billy can be a frustrated assistant coach." The blood in the coaching fraternity runs thick and the two basic commandments say don't rap the college game or a coach. As it turned out, Packer later answered to NBC officials for his fun.

Before the Tulane game, January 10, Digger talked about the bond that had developed between his players, drawing them closer in tough times. He also mentioned Packer's comments. It wasn't the first time he and the Notre Dame program were criticized, he said, and it wouldn't be the last. But Digger wanted to put the situation in perspective for his men. They were members of the Notre Dame basketball family and they too had been indirectly criticized. It was time to turn the negative article into a positive factor in the team's development. If there was a point in the season where the team could go into a slide, the Tulane game could be it, so Digger had to remotivate his team.

"No matter how many games we lose or how many games we blow out or steal at the buzzer," he said, "it still all gets back to two things: loyalty and family." He turned to Woolridge as an example. "Orlando, you could have gone to LSU, Tulane, Texas, or Oklahoma. But you chose to go to Notre Dame." Digger recalled that three years earlier the coaching staff hadn't even known about Woolridge or his basketball talents. Former New York Knick star Willis Reed, Orlando's second cousin, had informed Digger of this diamond in the rough. The coaches gambled, Orlando gambled, and the rest went into the Notre Dame record books. Phelps pointed out to the rest of the team how Woolridge progressed as a player and person, fighting through some difficult moments when his success could have gone to his head. "Tonight I hope you just have forty great minutes out there, Orlando."

Digger also reminded the team that it was part of the public life that accompanies Notre Dame athletics. "People second-guess and that's human nature. People are always going to take shots at you. That's just public life and that's a position we're in because we're Notre Dame. Those people are either jealous or they just don't understand what you are and the goals you're striving for."

Concluding, Digger pointed out how the team could distinguish itself now, reminding the players of a 1929 national championship plaque in the arena lobby. "You guys have got to somehow believe that you can make that happen, that you can give enough. Let's go out and capture that intensity that we've lacked since the Northwestern game. Set your own game tempo with execution and solid team defense."

The first half wasn't artistic but the Irish played well enough to lead, 34–27. Orlando was jittery before the home crowd, but he also displayed the concentration at the free-throw line that Digger had stressed. "The Tree" sank six free throws in six tries, then finally displayed his awesome leaping talents with a slam dunk in the closing minute of the half. Notre Dame's shooting percentage had improved drastically from the field, rising to a more healthy 48 percent. Tulane closed the margin in the first few minutes of the second half. At one point the Hirsch Memorial Coliseum became frenzied as the Green Wave took the lead, 42–40, six minutes into the final stanza. It was from that point that the Irish left the basketball blues behind, awakening from their mini-slump and proceeding to pull away from Tulane, finishing with a twenty-point victory of 79–59.

Digger summed it all up: "We played good half-court defense and we played with steam." He was happy with the team's response to the mental challenge of the newspaper article and the physical challenge of Tulane.

Following the game there was an alumni gathering for the team and then the nomads were off to San Antonio to learn how the real West was won.

The Hicks Dude Ranch provided the Irish ballplayers with a view of western life. The entire traveling party, including wives, writers, and school officials, spent an entire day on the ranch, enjoying the hospitality of Randy Hicks, whose daughter, Kelly, played on the Notre Dame women's basketball team. The visitors got to taste the dust of a trail, sample a true Texas barbecue, and even experience the joy of riding high in the saddle. The players and coaches sported cowboy hats to fit in with the western atmosphere. Digger has found a spot where his cowboy hats were commonplace. One of the highlights for the tourists occurred when it came time to do some riding. The leggy members of the club resembled frogs set to leap, as the stirrups, stretched downward to their limit, were not long enough to compensate for the legs of Woolridge, Andree, and Hanzlik. "But each kid did it his own way," Digger said later. "Just as each one displayed a unique style of play on the court, the same individuality carried over into riding horses." For Stacy Russo, the senior manager, the riding experience almost never started. Stacey climbed aboard his horse—who didn't stir despite considerable coaxing; obviously the animal didn't realize the rider's position of authority. Stacy's manager crew always snapped into action at his command; eventually he persuaded the horse to walk a few feet.

When the team finally got back to San Antonio it was late Saturday night. The dude ranch had been a rare experience. It was a planned example of Digger's philosophy in coaching and life: there have to be escapes where you forget what you're doing and enjoy something special. But the time for playing cowboy was over now. There were seventeen games ahead, and the following day it would be back to the basketball court for a meeting with Texas Christian University.

Gilbert Salinas got a taste of what it's like to be a celebrity or a politician stopping off for a campaign address. The San Antonio native was given the full V.I.P. treatment. For the slender junior it was an emotional moment when he stepped off the aircraft and onto a red carpet rolled out especially for his arrival. The Chamber of Commerce was making sure its contribution to the Notre Dame basketball program was treated well on his visit home. A band was there for the player affectionately called "the world's tallest Mexican"—who had trouble holding back his emotions. When it came time to introduce his parents, Gilbert simply choked up. But finally he managed to speak. In a soprano voice that seemed as high pitched as Gilbert is tall, the Salinas family was introduced. The HemisFair Arena crowd also welcomed their local boy back home with a three-minute standing ovation as Texas Anglos and Texas Mexicans welcomed not only Gilbert but his Irish teammates. For Gilbert, his parents, teammates, coaches, and anyone else there, it was an experience as important as winning a game.

It was also an on-court tonic for Salinas and his teammates. Tripucka and Jackson started quickly, after having split time between the bench and the court in the Tulane game of January 13. Hanzlik was also in action, beginning to regain his natural coordination after the injury layoff. The second five saw more playing time and took advantage of the chance to display their talents. Defensively the Irish held TCU to a mere twenty-six points, and led by 18 points in the first half. The rest of the contest was a learning experience for players like Paxson, Mitchell, Andree, and Varner, as Digger went through various strategies while working the entire squad. Final score: Notre Dame 85–TCU 68.

Salinas played particularly well before his hometown audience. Digger had recognized his capabilities on the team's trip to Yugoslavia the summer before. After going through some growing pains on and off the court, Gilbert was making his contribution in his own way. "I've learned that it takes Gil a little longer to come off an injury and get ready to play," said Digger after the game. "He also has tendencies not to worry or be concerned at times." This was true. As a sophomore Salinas had missed the second semester of basketball with grade problems. Notre Dame athletes have to maintain a 2.0 grade point average, four tenths above the NCAA's own requirement. Gil's academic eligibility boiled down to the difference between a B and a B-minus. It wasn't much of a distinction but the university rules said Salinas would have to miss the season's second half. There was no bending or twisting the rules for an athlete.

"It came down to a small distinction in one class," recalled Digger. "But the point I made with Gilbert was that he would not have been in that position if another C had been a B or a D a C.

That's an aspect of Gil's personality that still has to grow and that I'll try to help him with as the season develops."

The record of a winning basketball coach is not only a matter of scores and statistics.

10

STEALING A LITTLE MOMENTUM

Great teams do the right thing at the right time. They can be likened to champion prizefighters meeting talented challengers. The champion spars along, waiting for the upstart to punch himself out, then reaches back and delivers the knockout blow to insure the defense of his title. For the eighth-ranked Irish it was going to be that type of night. After four games on the road and three within five days it was a tired club that returned home to uphold its prestige on the home court against Villanova, January 15. Digger hoped the team would overcome the challenge by reaching back—like a ring champion—for that something extra.

Before the game Digger sat quietly in the locker room while the team warmed up on the A.C.C. floor, attempting to reacquaint itself with what had almost become foreign surroundings after the long road trip. While the players adjusted their shooting touches to the rims, the head coach rehearsed his pregame talk to the team, squatting on a stool next to the stereo and listening to the Marshall Tucker song, "Can't You See."

"I hope the players aren't as tired as I am," Digger said to an assistant, realizing fully that Villanova would be well coached by Rollie Massimino. The home-court edge would not be as much of a factor, he felt, because the Wildcats had nearly upset Notre Dame when they last visited South Bend two seasons before. Departed Irish guard Duck Williams, one of many Washington area players at Notre Dame, had notched two clutch freethrows to edge Villanova, 70–69. Digger calculated that knowledge and confidence would help Massimino instill a cockiness in his team and deflate any psych job the student body was capable of performing. "It's got to be a mental approach tonight," he said. "Our emotions will have to carry us through."

Now the team came in. "We're going to have our hands full tonight," Digger warned the players as they sat in front of their lockers. "Tonight is Villanova's UCLA game; they'll be ready to come at you after barely losing the last time they played here. You've got to be ready, on the court, during time outs, between foul shots, all the time. They'll be emotionally high, but it's up to us to be intense and blow them out. We've got to give them a lesson in intensity and being ready to play."

Other points had to be made. The NCAA's were looming on the horizon, and even closer was a rematch with UCLA four days away. But Digger warned the team not to look ahead. He also reminded each player that he could tolerate one or two mistakes, but a third mistake would earn the individual some time on the bench. "It's in here." Digger thrust his finger into his chest. "And it's in here." He gestured to his head. "That's how you play this ball game and if you go after Villanova like that they'll wish they were back in the Palestra."

Through the first fifteen minutes of the first half Notre Dame quickly learned that Villanova executed well and that Rollie Massimino rotated his defenses well enough to disrupt the Irish offense. After struggling along, Billy Hanzlik started the team on an eight-point spurt that boosted the Irish to a 32–24 lead at halftime. When Digger addressed the players during the intermission he built on that momentum, hoping it would carry over when the second half began.

"You weren't ready to start again," he said. "But the important point is that you bailed yourselves out—and that's a good sign." As he spoke he made adjustments, calling on assistant Scott Thompson to diagram a play he'd spotted from his position in the audio booth high above courtside. Thompson showed how the Irish could break the pressure defense that Villanova was applying over three quarters of the court. Digger was also busy diagramming plays on the blackboard as halftime slipped away. "Okay," he said, "You've got the lead and you know how to keep the momentum going. Don't give that lead away like you did against Tulane."

It looked as if the coaching staff was psychic. Thompson's adjustments helped break the pressure defense and the Irish coaches engineered leads of seventeen, fifteen, and then sixteen points. Another team might have folded, but the pudgy Massimino

continued to instill fire in his team as he discarded his coat and
rolled up his sleeves. It was going to come down to the last shot as
Rory Sparrow's jumper brought the Wildcats only one point behind,
68–67 with 0:41 left in regulation. Digger, Danny Nee, and Tommy
McLaughlin coached furiously as Tracy Jackson stepped to the line
for a one-and-one free-throw attempt. The shot could give the Irish a
two-point cushion with less than a minute left. It had been written
on the game card and on the blackboard before the game: "Make
your free throws." Jackson missed, Sparrow hit a layup with five
seconds, and Villanova was five seconds from the upset that had
slipped away from them two years back.

Sweat rolled down Digger's face as he diagrammed an
inbounds play that would hopefully bring the Irish the length of the
court and allow enough time for a shot. He positioned Woolridge
under the basket, Tripucka threw the ball in, and Wilcox, Branning,
and Jackson ran a series of picks that opened an alley for Jackson.
Tracy dribbled down the left side and swished a thirty-three footer
that ripped through the cords as the buzzer sounded. It was the
knockout punch that sent Villanova spinning to the canvas.

But it was Digger who looked like the victim of the battle as
he etched the team's shortcomings in their minds before the
moment escaped. Tossing off his coat, he stood before the team in a
sweat-drenched shirt. "To me tonight is like a loss," he said. "You
guys should have faith because faith won us the ball game tonight.
Tracy played great—he hit a hell of a shot to win it for us. But the
rest of you let us down in one way or another."

Digger then outlined each player's mistakes, going around
the locker room and remembering a bad shot, a gamble, or a
"dumb foul." Hanzlik had fouled out in twenty-four minutes. That
wasn't the type of leadership the coaches were counting on.

"You didn't quit and for that I'm thankful," said Digger, only to
add: "I'm concerned for this team right now; we're not playing the
way I think we're capable of playing." With that Digger huddled the
team together.

Then he turned to Jackson: "Tracy, that was a tremendous
shot. Now let's all of us sit and see where we're heading. Can't you
see?" And so saying, he instructed a manager to turn on the stereo
and play the song "Can't You See?"

After that, Digger headed for the press conference, then over to the Villanova locker room. Here, the players were staring at the floor; several wept silently. Digger had lost a few games at the buzzer himself and he felt it only right to tell the Wildcat players just that: "You guys deserved to beat us tonight—if that's any consolation."

Rollie Massimino was just as classy in defeat, calling Jackson's shot phenomenal. "You don't lose more than one out of a hundred like that," he told Digger. "This was the one."

Before Digger could leave for the West Coast and a national television game he had to make a trip to Armando's, a barber shop close to campus that attracted many of the Irish coaches and athletic officials. Whenever Digger had his hair cut, he and Armando always swapped verbal blows, one commenting on the terrible barbering and the other bewailing the poor coaching job done in a recent game. When the haircut was finished, Digger would remark, "This is great—now I can enroll in Officers Candidate School."

Armando also had the latest gossip about Notre Dame sports, whether football, basketball, or hockey. Stepping into Armando's was like leafing through old Notre Dame programs and press guides; an entire wall of the shop was covered with sports pictures mixed with autographed photographs of Irish coaches and players. The most important picture—that of Ara Parseghian—stood over the phone near Armando's chair. Parseghian always got his hair cut just before the shop opened for regular business. Armando was a Notre Dame tradition, and when his wife, Janet, gave birth to a son on January 17th, Digger arranged a special gift for the child: a letter on Notre Dame basketball stationery, attached to an actual basketball grant-in-aid bearing the name of Armando Jeffrey Femia for the school year 1998–99. It wasn't really a scholarship, but as usual, it was the thought that mattered.

Pauley Pavilion is to college basketball what the Boston Garden is to the National Basketball Association. Both symbolize a rich basketball tradition on their respective levels. Since the Bruins adopted Pauley Pavilion as their home only eight of their games had ended in defeat, in contrast to 226 victories. Maybe it was a stroke of luck, or maybe it was Digger Phelps's emphasis on the UCLA rivalry that resulted in Notre Dame winning an unprecedented trio of games from the Bruins on their home court. Even more amazing, the Irish were the first independent to beat the Bruins at home; only USC and Oregon had equaled the feat, and those teams had not managed three straight victories at Pauley as Digger's charges had. Now, with NBC commentators Dick Enberg, Al McGuire, and Billy Packer preparing to broadcast the confrontation coast to coast, Digger was seeking to direct his team to an unprecedented fourth victory in a row against UCLA in its hallowed home stadium, on January 19.

For Digger the spirit of the UCLA–Notre Dame contests epitomizes college basketball. When the home-and-home series moves west, game day starts with the band playing the fast-paced *William Tell* overture (better known these days as the Lone Ranger theme). As the music resounds through the empty arena the doors open and students burst in, urged on by the quickening tempo of the music. There are no reserved seats for UCLA students at Pauley; it's first come, first served. Digger makes sure he's around to watch the stampede of Californians as they streak for the best seats. That event almost sets the pace for the head coach. At the very least, it signals the start of the performance for Digger.

"The hostile crowd at Pauley has never really bothered our kids," he once said, "because I try to bring the attention down on me. If the crowd is on me, whether because I'm jumping around or getting on an official, it relieves some of the pressure on the team. I can handle the crowd better than a group of young players who get thrown into Pauley once a season."

And as Digger plays to the crowd at Pauley, the fans seem to interact with him, they in turn play to him—the man who seems to hold some type of mastery over the usually adept Bruins. Digger is greeted with hoots, jeers, and boos. Somehow he loves the attention and welcomes the chance to distract the spectators' attention from his players.

Digger began his pregame talk with the knowledge that he hadn't been too tough on the team—or as intense as he could have been about the UCLA clash. He was happy with the Villanova win even though he wouldn't let the team know it. Inwardly he realized the lift that Tracy's shot had given the players, rescuing them from upset and allowing the team to build momentum. Just the same, he felt that the players still weren't reading the situations and arriving at the outcomes he and the staff desired. He had to stress execution and concentration, an area of weakness that had almost cost them the game against Villanova. It was time to improve on that today and hopefully have Hanzlik in the game to run the team instead of on the bench as a result of the foul.

"We haven't peaked as a basketball team," he said. "We're not playing to our potential. UCLA has lost two in a row, but don't let that fool you. They'll be hungry for a win and you've got to be ready to play mean and smart. UCLA doesn't think you're that good. They think they should have beat you in South Bend because you give up easy baskets and don't play defense."

But it wasn't all scolding; morale had to be built up, too: "I think UCLA is going through a drought that we started at Notre Dame when we broke their eighty-eight–game winning streak. You guys added to that drought by beating them here at Pauley the last three years and now other teams aren't afraid of playing them—to the point where Arizona State beat them here Thursday night."

Then he got down to court strategy and tactics. He called for the defense to attack the UCLA players when they had the ball, shutting down the Bruins' running game. "Pressure them, man to man—they'll turn the ball over. I don't think they can handle the way we sequence our defenses.

"Offensively we've got to break their press. Keep your dribble and don't trap yourself." Larry Brown had the Bruins playing his run-and-jump defense and Digger wanted his players to handle it. "Remember, don't make any diagonal passes and make sure you read the defense before you throw a pass down the floor to your man. Against zones run the crossing patterns, and against man to man run the screen plays."

It was time to take the court, so Digger wound it up: "Baloney on a series split—we're going for a clean sweep!

"We need a big game, especially on the road," Phelps concluded. Just as he had done at the end of the Villanova game Digger played the Marshall Tucker song "Can't You See" to remind the team of their mistakes a few nights ago and to provide the message to the team. "You're good. Be patient and execute. It's that time of year again."

The team responded well to the crowd, going about its business in a patient manner and trailing UCLA by only two points after a sensational shot by Kiki Vandeweghe to end the half. Rich Branning, a native of nearby Huntington Beach, was on his way to another outstanding performance against UCLA. In his freshman appearance Rich had scored the last four points of the game to boost the Irish to a 66–63 win. From that game on Branning especially starred against the Bruins and this first half hadn't been much different. The well-groomed guard had hit all five of his shots and added two free throws. "You took away their offense," Digger exulted at the half. "We stole the momentum and if we do it for twenty more minutes we'll win."

The prediction stood as the intruding Irish worked their magic on the home court favorites. Ten minutes into the half Kelly Tripucka chucked in seven points as Notre Dame spurted to a 61–50 lead. Branning finished with twenty points, Jackson nineteen, and Kelly seventeen. It was a jubilant team that entered the locker room following their 80–73 win. All but Woolridge.

"Orlando, why are you pouting?" asked Digger after the team assembled. Woolridge quietly denied that he was, but Digger said, "You're certainly not smiling." Nor was he. It had not been the best of his nights against Vandeweghe, as he had scored a mere four points while snaring three rebounds.

"See, that's what tears it all down," explained Phelps in a fatherly manner. "So what, you had a bad night," said Digger. "You got screwed on a few calls but you should be celebrating." Woolridge said, "Oh, I will be." " 'O', I wish you were that smart on the court," replied Digger.

For four straight years Notre Dame had defeated UCLA at home. For walk-ons Marc Kelly and Kevin Hawkins it was especially worth delaying their return to campus so that they could suit up for their first UCLA game at Pauley Pavilion. Because they don't travel with the team, the pair usually misses the second half of the epic battle. But fortunately, because of the Christmas break, the two California residents were able to stay home a few extra days and schedule their flights back to campus after the game.

Before the players left, Digger revealed a plan, something to reinforce the four straight victories. "Don't tell the media, but we're going to get a green banner of our own to hang up with the rest of the NCAA championship banners," he said.

After the stretch of road games Notre Dame was getting ready for a home stand, playing seven of eight games at the A.C.C.; the series would carry the team into February. Upcoming were some big games against the likes of Maryland–January 26, North Carolina State–February 9, and San Francisco–February 11, plus a single road game against LaSalle at Philadelphia's Palestra–January 30. "Practice games" were also scheduled against Davidson–February 2, Navy–February 4, Manhattan–February 6, and Canisius–January 23.

Canisius is a small Catholic university from Buffalo, New York; the Irish hadn't faced its team since 1961. Now, before the 1980 game, Scott Thompson hastily walked the team through the Canisius offense and defensive patterns in an empty auxiliary gymnasium. Earlier in the day the team had watched the films of the UCLA game as the coaches pointed out miscues. Digger was upset about a player questioning a referee; that would stop in future games, he said. Later, before a relaxed group, he set the tone of the game.

"I want each of you guys to think back to a weakness you spotted in yourself against UCLA and try to correct it tonight," he instructed. "Do the little things on defense; get your hand in the shooter's face." He did not want his team to start lackadaisically, either, and told the players, "We haven't pounded anyone all year; let's do it tonight."

Notre Dame didn't exactly pound their guests in the first half, but their effort was enough for a thirteen-point lead. It was another night where the Irish weren't quite at full strength. Woolridge was sitting out the game with an infected heel and Gil Salinas started at center. If there was a problem in the first half it was that the second wave squandered a fourteen-point lead down to eight. Digger therefore spent quite a bit of the halftime at the blackboard, instructing the second five in execution. The team responded better in the second twenty minutes and finished with an 84–63 win that included ten points by freshman Bill Varner, who saw a little more action in the front line than usual. Phelps made sure to encourage Billy about the way he reacted to his role, coming in to do the job for the laid-up Woolridge.

There were signs that Varner might also see more action that weekend as Tripucka complained of a soreness in his back—that had been reflected in a three-for-five shooting performance. The next day Kelly flew out for a New Jersey awards dinner where he received the state's Amateur Athlete of the Year distinction. Digger wasn't too happy about Kelly taking off for his home state; it was a distraction in the scheme of the season. He was glad Kelly was being honored, of course, but he felt the dinner could have come after the season. As fate would have it, his misgivings were well founded.

On the Friday afternoon before the Maryland game, NBC commentators, technical directors, and producers were scrambling about in the basketball arena while the Irish ran through a few last-minute preparations. McGuire and Enberg were watching the workout as they did their homework for the broadcast the next day. There was a sense of anticipation similar to the electricity in the air on a fall Friday before a home football game. Outside the A.C.C. it was difficult to sense the activity on the South Bend campus, the harsh Indiana winter having long ago sent Notre Dame students into their dormitories. The noticeable movement outdoors was restricted to trips to class, a hockey game, and maybe a trip down Notre Dame Avenue to Goose's, Corby's, or Nickie's, three student bars near campus. The college slowed, but did not stop for winter— something the Maryland team had learned in its last visit to South Bend.

In 1978 the Terps' charter flight was one of the last planes to land at the Michiana Regional Airport before thirty-six inches of snow blanketed the community in less than fourteen hours. South Benders remember the Blizzard of '78 well. It closed roads and emptied grocery store shelves as people were told to stay off the roads for almost three days while snowplow crews attempted to open the public thoroughfares. Neighbors walked to each other's homes for parties that will long be remembered while private encounters produced a boom for doctors the following October. Since Maryland and NBC had arrived, Notre Dame officials decided the game should go on as scheduled. But because only Civil Defense teams were allowed on the roads, Irish fans could not drive to the game and many ticket holders settled for the television broadcast instead. For residents within walking distance, the blizzard opened the A.C.C. doors. Anyone who could walk to the game was admitted free and the result was a thunderous crowd that inspired Notre Dame to a 69–54 victory. Coach Lefty Driesell left town shuddering, aboard the first bus allowed on the Indiana Toll

Road. Fortunately, however, winter spared the visitors a repeat weather performance on their return in 1980.

Practice was going smoothly when another injury struck the Irish. Kelly Tripucka writhed with a lower back pain that divided doctor's opinions between back spasms or kidney stones. With Kelly leaving the court on a stretcher, Digger's relaxed manner soon reverted to an all-business approach. He would need Salinas and Varner ready to step into the front line and play against the Atlantic Coast Conference's number-one team. As practice progressed, trainer Skip Meyer had the difficult chore of estimating Kelly's injury for Digger. The treatments to relax the muscles in the lower back hadn't been effective and it looked as if Tripucka would definitely be sidelined for the game. Without being close enough to hear Meyer's words, the context of the message was visible in Digger's expression. It was another handicap for the team to overcome; the squad would have to adjust to the absence of their All-America forward and defeat the Terps without his help. Digger could not help putting some of the blame on the planners of the New Jersey awards dinner: if it had been organized at a better time, Kelly would not have spent several hours cramped in the restricting seats of a commercial airliner. But, what was done was done, and Digger could not afford to spend time dwelling on the loss. He had told the team it had the ability to overcome injuries and still win games back in November when Hanzlik underwent surgery. Here was another injury that could be a rallying point—or an adverse element. Digger would have to figure how to work around it later, after the practice and after the pep rally set for the auxiliary gymnasium.

The rallies, instituted by Digger a few years earlier, usually drew modest crowds in the gymnasium nicknamed "The Pit" for its sunken position between the twin domes. It had become a custom for the players with seniority to address the crowd. Digger says it's their turn for the limelight after paying their dues.

With the Notre Dame Marching Band present to break into the Fight Song at the opportune moment, Billy Hanzlik stood sandwiched between the cheerleaders and addressed the gathering. The senior from Wisconsin told the crowd that Digger was going after his 200th career win against Maryland and that the team wouldn't disappoint their coach or their fans. Digger squirmed in his seat and looked at his assistants. He would have preferred to keep the 200th-win item quiet, as it could be something Lefty Driesell might be able to work into a pregame talk to his Terps. But, it was too late for secrecy. And besides, Digger would have much on his mind the next day, with Tripucka in St. Joseph's Hospital.

If there was any thread of hope that Kelly would play it was erased Saturday morning. As the players gathered after the team mass, one member of the family lay in a hospital bed, resigned to watching his teammates' efforts on television. Gil Salinas, the senior, and Bill Varner, the freshman, were going to have to make significant contributions. Digger began his game comments in an encouraging manner, realizing he couldn't afford to be too harsh on this occasion. There were times when he would challenge the player's pride, but this wasn't one of those times. Kelly's absence presented the team with a challenge each player could understand without a pep talk. So Digger simply painted the game plan and strategy in a casual manner, setting the stage, but not adding to the nervousness of Salinas and Varner, who would be burdened enough by Tripucka's absence.

"Maryland is ready. They're fired up and the last thing on their mind is the Atlantic Coast Conference," said Digger. "They'll get back to the conference Wednesday, but right now Lefty's in there getting them fired up to play the I-rish." Digger mimicked Driesell's drawn-out southern dialect. He also went back to the building blocks that had contributed to the team's growing momentum: patience, hard work, concentration. There were details, too. Digger's trio of coaches had scouted the Terps well and had plenty of advice for individuals, be it sagging off Butch Morley and Reggie Jackson or not reacting to Albert King's tendency to pump-fake. It was technical; it was specific and almost clairvoyant.

"Maryland will get hot at some point—they do it in every game they play," said Digger. "Just be patient; we'll change defenses and disrupt their tempo. Our four corners or delay sequences will bother them and we can take advantage of their tendency to be lazy after they score a basket."

"Yes, Maryland is a good basketball team," assessed Phelps of the visitor's talent. "The thing you have to believe is that you're better ... and that you'll win."

If the game had been judged by its first twenty minutes the two teams would come out even. The six lead changes indicated both teams played tight defense. Driesell and Digger labored through every minute of play, each struggling for an upper hand. It was another classic match-up between a big conference school and the big independent. With a twenty-foot jumper by John Paxson to end the half, the Irish trailed Maryland by a single point. Hanzlik had held Albert King to four points, a strong defensive effort, while Tracy Jackson and Woolridge hit eight apiece to provide the bulk of the Irish scoring. Tracy, who lived near the Maryland campus and even attended religious services with Driesell, always played well against the Terps. The halftime box score indicated that Driesell was going with six players while Digger worked everyone into the game but his walk-ons. The Terps shot 44 percent from the field while the Irish were dismal at 38.7 percent.

In the locker room, Digger stressed adjustments and better offensive execution, pointing out that the shots would start to fall in the second half if the team maintained its patient execution. "The thing to keep in mind is that they can't play any better and we can," he said. "The momentum is ours—keep it and we'll win."

The seesaw struggle continued in the last twenty minutes as the lead changed hands nine more times. Albert King finally lived up to Al McGuire's expectations and turned on for seventeen points to give his teammates a 63–62 lead with fifteen seconds left.

But now, as if lightning struck twice in the two weeks, Tracy Jackson snatched the game away from his hometown rivals with a driving layup with six seconds left. Driesell immediately called time out to prepare his team for one more shot. It was clear he'd go to King, his player with the hot hand. Digger didn't leave anything to chance by waiting until Maryland lined up on the court and then calling time out. The alignment suggested that King would get the ball, so Hanzlik was assigned to guard him. King got the pass at the Irish foul line, dribbled, and then pulled up to fire a jump shot at half court. Hanzlik leaped as high as he could and with outstretched arms pointing high in the air, forced King to cock back and disrupt his rhythm. The shot missed and Notre Dame chalked up another squeaker, 64–63.

"Thanks for my two-hundredth win, guys," said the relieved Digger in the locker room. "I was nervous about the game, and you certainly didn't help things. You're killing me." He laughed. "But you're unbelievable, too."

For two visiting recruits it must have been an education.

Digger turned the floor over to football coach Bill Meyers, who introduced Ken Jackson, a football and basketball player from South River, New Jersey, where Joe Theismann had played his high school football. "He's thinking about USC and Penn State," said Digger, "but after today he's got to want to join us here at the Dome."

Also present was highly regarded Glenn Rivers, a high school guard from Chicago. "Glenn is considering us along with De Paul and Marquette," Digger told the team. "Glenn, if you don't believe in this place after today, we're going to love playing against you." The team burst into laughter.

Now the players gathered around Digger for the final prayer. Digger held his hand out and the men placed their own hands over his, as he said, "Somebody up there loves us, but please let us make our foul shots." Then he told the players, "Pray for each other, and for those who need our prayers. And go down to the hospital, visit Kelly, and bring him a six pack."

La Salle would be the next opponent on the road in Philadelphia. The Irish would need more than prayers there.

11

TASTING DEFEAT

The Palestra was as much a part of Digger's initiation as a college coach as it was a cornerstone of Philadelphia basketball history. The creaky floors and the soft rims of the ancient gymnasium could tell many stories of great contests. And the La Salle game that night would be a heroic tale for the Explorers in 1980.

The Explorer team was a shadow of what it could have been. With forward Michael Brooks, the team should have done better than its 10–6 record as it entered the Irish matchup. Digger sized up the opponent by calling the Explorers "experienced players who have never beat you." He compared them to St. John's a year earlier, the team that was 9–8 before putting it together and barely missing a trip to the Final Four. Digger also recalled the games he'd seen at the Palestra as an assistant coach at Penn, hoping a little past history would help the players realize the significance of the Palestra and their opponent.

"A lot of top ten teams have come into the Palestra and lost to La Salle, Penn, Villanova, Temple, and St. Joseph's," he said. "Tonight La Salle is waiting to ambush you and it's going to take a strong mental approach to win it. If the crowd here tonight smells an upset, they'll root like hell for La Salle because they're starved for a win."

Digger went into the game plan, which included stopping the Explorers' transition game and forcing them to setup, pressuring rebounders and hitting the offensive boards. Doing that, plus shooting 90 percent from the foul line and playing hard for an entire game, would do it, said Digger. "Tonight you should get a good spring off the floor and take advantage of rims that are like sieves. You don't beat UCLA and Maryland and then lose to ten-six La Salle."

Despite those words the Irish tried their best to contradict Digger. La Salle opened the game by hitting six shots in a row. The

Irish then rushed to catch up at the other end. The result was a pathetic first half. Digger hardly had to remind the men of this in the locker room, but he did: "Every guy made a mistake out there." Salinas's play was especially displeasing, and Digger tried to ignite his first-line substitute, who was still filling in for the injured Tripucka. "Gil, you played nine minutes and you didn't even contribute any points. We need you to play, not pussyfoot." Digger also told the team, repeatedly, to think about its mistakes and then correct them in the second half. "And forget about any help from the referees—you won't be getting any. So go out and do it yourself."

Still, the hasty style of play continued in the second half, and the final margin of defeat for the Irish was 62–60. Digger found no consolation in being edged by a mere basket. To him, the loss signified a lack of concentration and a disregard for a capable team. Notre Dame had begun the game riding an emotional high from the Maryland victory—but against La Salle there was no spectacular shot to steal a victory. Digger felt his team had let momentum slip away as they joked around in the locker room while waiting to get the game over with. "We didn't maintain the concentration we had in previous games," he said. "The Maryland win left us on a cloud and we were still celebrating the victory while La Salle was ready and waiting." All the elements of an upset were there. The Explorers had hustled from the tip-off and never quit, hitting the key shots and playing well enough to nose out Digger's crew. Missed shots were something Digger could tolerate, but a breakdown in the mental part of the game would arouse his anger. The next day he would make sure the team realized how and why they had been ambushed in the Palestra.

It was the last day in the month of January and the atmosphere in the locker room suggested it was the last day of the world. Danny Nee was watching a videotape of the La Salle game, taking notes on plays he intended to point out when the team watched it later the next afternoon. The Brooklynite found himself upset by a few of the referee's calls in the game. The Palestra wouldn't be a pleasant memory of the season.

Next door, Digger was in a closed-door meeting with co-captains Branning and Hanzlik. It was unusual that Digger's door was closed. Normally there was heavy traffic in and out of the corner suite. The head coach's office was decorated in early Notre Dame, with countless mementos of Digger's career; curiosity seekers would poke their heads around the corner of the door to see the museum within. Today, though, Digger wanted to do some leveling with his two leaders. The team hadn't responded to the staff's instructions in Philadelphia and the head coach had to straighten out his "family" right away.

Later, as the players went through the taping ritual before practice, the coaching staff assembled in the locker room and Digger talked for the next thirty minutes about the team, its attitudes, and the way he felt the players were being sidetracked from the goal they should be jointly seeking: a national championship. "I don't know if we're really a family," he began. "I don't know if each one of you has made a commitment to winning that national championship or if you're just becoming selfish.

"I don't want you guys thinking, 'I'm getting screwed—I could do better than this guy, he stays in longer, or I need a chance.' If you're thinking that, you're thinking only about yourself; responding to pressure from your parents, your peers, or some other distraction. Don't be bothered when somebody in the dorm comes up to you and says 'You should be playing more.' All it can do is distract us from what we want to accomplish as a *team*. You have to make the best of three minutes or twenty minutes.

"Orlando, after I called time out, after I tried to be a nice guy with you, I chewed your ass out. I did it in front of the team and probably in front of the people sitting behind us and then you went out and played your heart out for three great minutes. That shows me it's mental and that you have the potential to be a Michael Brooks. I saw something inside you that even Michael Brooks doesn't have, I saw fire in your eyes—and now I expect it every minute I have you in the game. But sometimes every one of you guys gets in his own block and becomes distracted. Then I have to motivate you and, like it or not, I will.

"I see things that go on in a game, X's and O's. You men would see them, too, if you'd been coaching for fifteen years. But you haven't, so I want you to listen—and concentrate. We're not sitting here to BS; we're in here for a mental practice."

Digger referred to the previous night's pregame talk as a "comedy hour." It was always easy to get motivated in Pauley Pavilion or against Maryland, he said, but La Salle, with its 10–6 record, was a different challenge. He pointed out how each La Salle player contributed to the win with inspired play, contrasting it to the breakdown of the Irish players in key situations. "La Salle got a big zip and then developed the confidence they needed to beat us. They said 'Hey, Notre Dame's overrated.' And we *are,* when we don't play to our potential."

The bench came in for evaluation. It hadn't played well, shooting a mediocre 30 percent. Digger drew an analogy of a designated hitter fouling off the first two pitches and then taking a called third strike. "He can't ask for a fourth strike or for batting practice. He's got a role, and some of your roles are just like a designated hitter's. Come off the bench ready."

Digger then went around the room and discussed each player's attitude. "Mitch is mad because he's not playing more and I know damn well that when Tracy goes to the bench he's mad. That's what kills us, worrying about playing time and I'm not singling you out, Tracy—this is just one case."

He went on down the roster. "Orlando, you be a Michael Brooks. You're overdue, so let's see that fire in your eyes whenever you're on the court.

Stan: You're in a slump, but you're playing positive. You can't get any lower—the next step is up. Play defense and be a clutch ballhandler. Points are a bonus as far as I'm concerned.

Gilbert: You're playing well in spurts, but you've got to be more consistent. You have the talent to be our best shooter from the point. Work on toughening up and playing physical.

Tim [Healy]: You've just got to learn to suck it up, know your assignments in practice, and don't play shuck and duck when you get in a game.

Hawk: Just be ready to play and work hard in practice, just like Tim....

Varner: Forget about any distractions. You gave us ten great minutes in the Maryland game and played your best against La Salle. Just remember that when Kelly comes back it's his turn, but yours will come."

The players were silent as Digger went to the water cooler. Then he cleared his throat; he hadn't finished his individual evaluations.

Tim [Andree]: You're our biggest player and you've got to take up room in the middle for us. I think you have more potential than Laimbeer and Flowers combined. Think of your development as if you were an assembly line worker in Detroit building a car. Make me a Cadillac Seville, but if it takes twelve hours, do it in fourteen hours instead of rushing. Then, the next one you make will take only eleven hours and improve that way, slowly. Freshman centers aren't usually able to dominate, so don't get down on yourself. Kent Benson was horrible as a freshman.

Mike: Just play your best when you're in there, take your shots when they're there. I can't make time guarantees so it's up to you to be consistent when you're in the game.

Rich: You're in a shooting slump so just shoot out of it. Work on consistency and continue to be a leader.

Marc: Accept getting in there for a minute if we're trying to experiment with some different looks at the end of the game. Even though we may be winning, I might be trying something for the next game. Have fun by executing, but play the way we teach you....

Hanz: Play under control and smart. Quick shots and that jump-hook kill us. You're our mental leader, so push us....

Tracy: You're in a great offensive groove. Don't force shots, though. Just keep doing it like you've been doing it....

Pax: Just keep making things happen when you're in there. Don't dribble in traffic and leave it up to me to decide when you go in....

Kelly: Get healthy and start over. Build me a Seville and play defense while you're doing it."

When Digger finished he gave the players a chance to respond. With the mental part of practice over it was time to reflect on the court session. A college basketball season almost spans six months and Digger knew it was easy to succumb to distractions along the way. His talk, he hoped, was a refresher course. Now it was up to the players to do their own homework and pass the test.

12

DOG DAYS OF FEBRUARY

Early February started the Irish on a five-game home stand that kicked off with a trio of contests leading up to the likes of North Carolina State and San Francisco. Although Davidson, Navy, and Manhattan were not top-twenty caliber, the stretch would give the coaching staff the opportunity to get the team back on the winning track while working on some pages of the playbook that were't being executed effectively. Digger hoped the three games would be both a learning experience and a recuperation period for the walking wounded. The Irish were in the final month of the regular season; it was time to put it all together in the eleven games leading up to the tournament.

The goal for the Davidson game was clear: learn by defeat and turn it into a win. That afternoon many of the coaches and players watched NBC's broadcast of the Ohio State–Wisconsin game, where the powerful Buckeyes were edged by the upstart Badgers. "Ohio State blew an eleven-point lead and lost by three points today, guys," said Digger in his pregame remarks. "That shows there's a big part of this game that's mental." He also reminded the men of the gloomy locker-room scene in Philadelphia three nights before, and spelled out the attitude he wanted to observe from his kneeling position in front of the bench.

"Don't be looking around for any excuses tonight, or someone else to blame," he warned. "If something goes wrong, look inside yourself and say 'It's my fault.' Go out tonight and just kick some ass. Don't wait for me to call time out to tell you how badly you're playing. I think you stink, so go out on that court mad and hungry for a victory."

That last jolted the players. But Digger wasn't done yet.

"I want you to capitalize on the experiences you're getting here at Notre Dame," he said. "As basketball players you receive more opportunities than other students and you've got to make the most of them so that your success can continue when you graduate. I don't care what type of career you want—what you get here at Notre Dame will help you. Even if you're a philosopher sitting on a bench in Central Park and the pigeons are crapping on you, be the best bum there. If you don't try to be the best, people will walk all over you when you're trying to get that sales account or win that court case ... just like La Salle walked all over you three nights ago."

Phelps huddled the team at just the right time. Ed O'Rourke, the devoted Irish basketball fan, had all he could do to keep from laughing and John Paxson was near smiling, too. Later Digger laughed, too, when he and O'Rourke told Roger Valdiserri about the speech. It was obvious Pat O'Brien would never have immortalized those words of Digger's in a movie, as he had with Rockne's "Win one for the Gipper" speech. But Digger had felt that his hard-line approach was worth a try.

It was indeed. Davidson felt Notre Dame's—and Digger's—wrath for an entire forty minutes as the players worked the frustration of losing out of their systems. The rout began with four straight Irish baskets and finished with Tim Healy feeding Bill Varner for a slam dunk to cap a 105–71 trouncing. The final margin was the biggest bulge of the year for Notre Dame and also the first time the club exceeded the 100-point plateau. Davidson Coach Eddie Biedenbach summed it up: "Notre Dame came out ready to kill us."

Digger had done a good job sizing up the emotional factors of the game and the players had been no less successful in executing his game plan. And two nights later they awaited their chance to continue the learning game and their momentum. The squad from the Naval Academy presented the team with a different challenge. The players in the Irish locker room were told to be ready for frustration tactics from a disciplined squad. Digger calculated that the Middies' military regimentation would carry over to their style of play. "Expect a delay game and remember to play smart," he cautioned.

The team also received an impromptu lesson in foul-shooting. Digger wanted the players to be sharp from the charity line when it came down to sinking foul shots, should Navy opt for fouling to get the ball coupled with a possible stall. Digger flipped a locker-room stool upside down to illustrate a point about the actual size of the basket; it was a mental gimmick to instill the impression of a large target to shoot for from the foul line. While Stacy Russo tracked down a couple of basketballs for the demonstration, Digger explained the art.

"Just use enough trajectory to get the ball on the top of the rim," he said. "If you do that the ball will work its way through the net as it comes down. Give it the space it needs: the lower the shot the less trajectory and the slimmer the chances of making it."

Stacy arrived with the balls and Digger set the pair inside the bottom ring of the stool. "See how small this stool is? But there's plenty of room for two basketballs, and the backboard rims are even bigger than that. Just push the ball up, grab for the rim to get it there straight, and if it's up there it's going to drop." At times that rim would look awfully small, especially in the closing minutes of a tight game.

But the Irish had thirty-eight opportunities to practice Digger's theory, and successfully converted twenty-nine free throws for a .763 mark. The 67–53 final score was good enough for Digger, even though Navy had played methodically, forcing the Irish into what Digger called "sloppy execution." Still, he wanted the team to continue the season in an upbeat frame of mind.

"Don't be upset with the way you played tonight or what you did wrong," he told the men. "A disciplined team forced you into making those mistakes. Now just learn from them."

Manhattan coach Brian Mahoney wasn't smiling when the team entered the A.C.C; his Jaspers must have felt like the Christians in the days of ancient Rome when the Colosseum games were about to start. Mahoney's first year as Manhattan's coach was as dismal as Digger Phelps's start at Notre Dame, and following the 6–20 season the young New York coach found his starting five decimated by graduation. Unfortunately, Mahoney's second season began with losing two returning players to academic problems. Without two would-be starters his estimation of the team was "not very deep." For Mahoney, the year developed into an even greater study in frustration than his first season.

With that situation in mind, Digger set out to motivate his men to play hard against a team that had managed only two wins. Digger had a twinge of compassion for the struggling Mahoney, knowing all too well the pressures Brian was no doubt facing. Still, he had no intention to improve Manhattan's season at the expense of the continuity his own players were struggling to develop. Injuries had already become a factor in their season; tonight Tripucka would be back in the lineup for the first time in four games, while Salinas would also get a chance to test a slight ankle sprain that had forced him out in the second half of the Navy game. The bumps and bruises were minor yet potentially damaging.

A few days earlier, Digger and many of the players had watched the second game of the Notre Dame–Wisconsin hockey competition, and Digger now decided to borrow a situation or two from the other Athletic and Convocation Center tenant. Digger was no stranger to ice hockey. His son Rick played defense and sometimes forward in the local Irish Youth Hockey League, and the Notre Dame varsity hockey games gave him a chance to observe even more. The Saturday before, Irish hockey coach Lefty Smith had matched Digger's record with his own 200th career victory at the university; but Sunday's game had slipped away when the Badgers did something Digger wanted to teach his own players.

"When Wisconsin was trailing four-one, they were still under control; they didn't panic and they waited for the chances," he said. The next sequence was what interested Phelps, a change in momentum that he and WNDU-TV sportscaster Jeff Jeffers predicted as they watched from the corner of the press box, munching hot dogs.

"Then one of our defensemen lost control of the puck and Wisconsin capitalized on the mistake—scored a goal on the play and then came back to win the game. That's what I want you guys to develop—a killer instinct, so you can capitalize on the other team's mistakes."

Digger also borrowed a baseball situation. If a team with a man on first needed one run to win, he said, it would be smart to advance him to second with a bunt, then single to score him or at least advance him to third, where a sacrifice fly would bring him in. He visualized a player telling his manager, "'I can hit the three-hundred footer.' I'd tell him, 'I know you can, but I still want a bunt.' Then, it's up to you to say 'Digger's the manager and if he wants a bunt, I'll do it to advance the runner.' But sometimes you guys swing for the fences, when all I want is a bunt, a walk, or a single."

Without the services of co-captain Rich Branning, the Irish set about to bunt, steal, and squeeze their way to victory. Manhattan was outmanned and outclassed, trailing 44–18 after the first twenty minutes, and finally dropping still another game, 93–49. Kelly Tripucka turned in as good an effort as anyone, hitting six of seven shots from the floor despite a "shaky" three-for-seven mark at the charity stripe. Orlando Woolridge also continued to star at his center position, proving himself a versatile athlete capable of making the transition from forward to center in the course of a season. Since the La Salle game "O" had streaked to twenty-, eighteen-, and fifteen-point performances—exhibiting the "fire" Digger had demanded from him.

The Jaspers' forty-nine–point output was the lowest total for an Irish opponent all season, rivaling a January 6, 1968, defensive record when Air Force managed forty-five points. Mahoney mixed frustration with praise for Notre Dame's players. He mentioned the national TV exposure the Irish received: The Metro Communications Network and NBC's telecasts were evident, too. "Our kids really wanted to play; they see Notre Dame all the time and they know Kelly and Stan from home." But he added, "I'm sure Digger doesn't want to play a team like us. I don't want to come here again if it keeps going the way it has. Every one of their players is very talented; we're just not ready for a team like that."

Notre Dame had now polished off three teams in five days and the coaches sensed the growing character of the team. On Sunday North Carolina State would test the Irish with a quick running game led by Hawkeye Whitney, and Digger predicted that Branning and Tripucka would be back in the starting lineup. It was time to go back to the arrangement the staff had adopted in the fall meetings—which seemed like ancient history now.

The Athletic and Convocation Center had been kind to the Irish, allowing them to build a home-court winning streak of fourteen contests against the likes of the Soviet Nationals, Villanova, UCLA, and Maryland—impressive programs that demanded respect on the college basketball scene. Notre Dame losses on the home court are as frequent as solar eclipses; twenty-five defeats spanned a dozen seasons, nine of them in Digger's first season and three more in 1972–73. Losing did more than disappoint the spectators; it sparked disgruntled remarks and waves of second-guessing throughout the A.C.C.'s padded and bleacher seats. Notre Dame's rich football tradition spoiled Notre Dame students, Notre Dame alumni, and Notre Dame fans everywhere. Losing opened the door to criticism of player performances, recruiting, and most of all, coaching. The spirit of college athletics sometimes took a back seat in spectator thinking as players were unfairly looked on in the same light as professional athletes. After ten years of college coaching, Digger was thick skinned when it came to attacks on his coaching style. His record spoke for itself, and bearing the brunt of the blame came with the job as far as he was concerned. But criticism of any Irish player was off limits: student athletes eighteen to twenty-one years old did not deserve amateur judgments based on professional standards. But before the North Carolina game was over Digger and his players would come under the heavy fire from the sports world's armchair centers, forwards, and guards. The A.C.C. streak was about to end.

The Wolfpack trailed Maryland in the Atlantic Coast Conference, but it still held the distinction of being the only ACC team to defeat Driesell's troops. As for their past performances against Notre Dame, Norm Sloan's charges had lost the last two games, and they badly wanted to rectify that situation. Perhaps the most eager was All-ACC forward Hawkeye Whitney, whose lackluster efforts had contributed to those two losses. Hawkeye entered the Saturday night contest averaging nearly twenty points per game, and Digger knew that his team's top-priority assignment would be to keep Hawkeye from "turning on."

"A win by North Carolina State tonight won't do them any good in the conference," Digger told his men in the locker room, "but it will build their confidence and their chances of receiving an at-large invitation to the tournament." Digger knew just what to expect, and warned of North Carolina's long-range shooting ability, together with a tendency to crash the boards for rebounds. "If you're going to win you're going to need patience when you play defense, penetration from the guards, and a lot of patience on offense. And, most of all, you can't let Hawkeye get started."

For the Irish, the NCAA countdown continued with the tournament only four weeks away. "The next two games are just what we need to condition ourselves for the tournament schedule; NC State and San Francisco are two strong teams and we'll play them within three days," Digger prescribed. "DePaul isn't going out and getting ready like we are," he said of the nation's only undefeated team. With Tripucka starting for the first time in five games and Branning at full strength Digger told his team it was only the third time in the season they had been a healthy unit. The other times were against the Russians and UCLA's Bruins.

"Just play your roles tonight; don't compromise the team's goal for one of your own," he implored.

But Hawkeye did get started—and that finished the Irish.

Both teams posted below-average shooting performances in the first twenty minutes, partly due to some tough defense and partly due to some tough luck. Still, Notre Dame clung to a two-point lead, which Digger insisted could have been fourteen points if the team hadn't committed thirteen turnovers. "You had a bad half, but you did well enough to grab the lead," he said mildly. "Just be patient; you have to play with discipline." Digger also told the team it could only get better in the second half, but the words proved to be half-truths. Things got better for Tripucka, who exploded with seventeen points in the final twenty minutes. The trouble was that Hawkeye also got better, pumping in twenty-three points, while Kenny Mathews added eleven and Sidney Lowe thirteen. With under five minutes on the clock the Irish found themselves trailing, 49–36. Three time-outs later they felt the sting of losing at the A.C.C., 63–55—the widest margin since a 1974-75 defeat by Indiana. North Carolina State had shot the lights out, converting fifteen of twenty shots into field goals.

Digger didn't have much to say to the team. After the best performances he always found the words to fill three or five minutes, but at this time silence seemed to be the best means of communication. Tomorrow would be different.

But Digger did talk to the press. He praised Norm Sloan's disciplined squad, calling Hawkeye "awesome" and Clyde "the Glide" Austin "a true team player" who showed great control. Hawkeye also spoke; his comments were like sighs of relief. "I was kind of tight at the beginning," he said. "This game meant a lot to me personally. The last two years we lost to Notre Dame and I had a bad game both times. It feels real good to have won." Sloan, too, voiced pleasure that his star player had worked past the first-half jitters: "The game meant a lot to him because he knew he would never play here again." North Carolina had gotten its psychological lift. The Irish were a different story.

The team had much to do before the San Francisco rematch on Monday night. On Sunday afternoon the players and coaches sat down for a three-hour meeting that Digger defined as "letting it all hang out." The family talked about everything from personalities to substitution techniques, and at the end, Digger felt that each player left the locker room with a deep commitment to winning an NCAA title. For some it meant accepting the fact that they would be playing less. For other players it meant concentrating even more intensely on their roles on the court, whether offensive or defensive. For Digger it meant toning down his manner as the season wound down. The burning desire to win couldn't be allowed to backfire against his players.

Then, after the men had "let it all hang out" in the meeting, Notre Dame's president, the Reverend Theodore Hesburgh, provided an emotional tonic before he began celebrating mass for the team. Hesburgh kept it simple and to the point. "You're going to win the game; I'm not worried about you," he said. Phelps looked upon Hesburgh's inspiration as a standard to measure the problems of the team and his own life. "When he said you're going to win and talked about the other problems of the world it took our minds off basketball and onto the greater problems of the world," interpreted Digger. "It was unbelievable," said Digger afterwards, "how Father Hesburgh, with just those few words, could lift the entire team and give us the confidence that had begun to erode."

But if Father Hesburgh had helped Digger with Notre Dame's basketball program, the university president also sought Digger's help in another area. Notre Dame was concerned about how to proceed with women's athletics after the Title IX proposal became law. Universities were now required to spend equal proportions on women's athletics according to the Title IX Act passed by Congress. A moratorium had already been placed on all scholarship sports with the exception of football and basketball, meaning none of the other coaches could recruit any new team members for next year or offer grant-in-aids. Father Hesburgh sounded Phelps out on his opinion after there had been much bad press about the scholarship freeze and rumors that the hockey program might be dropped. Digger had already given the matter some thought and decided Notre Dame should go ahead with a first class women's basketball program complete with scholarships. "I think it would be great for the women at Notre Dame and I also think it could be competitive and possibly earn money at some point in its development," he expressed. In a time when college athletics were feeling a financial squeeze with travel expenses and increases in practically every budget category, the bottom line had to be a consideration. The pair discussed the possibility of both teams traveling together and playing double-headers with a common opponent. The two men mulled over each other's suggestions and recommendations until it came time to meet San Francisco and revenge a loss to the Dons the month before.

There wasn't much Digger had to say when the squad assembled around seven o'clock that night. His objectives for the San Francisco game were standard: discipline, controlling the boards, and playing the proper role. "They're cocky as they sit in that locker room," he told the team, "because they believe they can beat you just like they did in January in Oakland. As a team we have to get in our rhythm and fight together. Our record is sixteen and four and we haven't reached our potential. On Saturday we sucker-punched ourselves, so now let's put our minds together. If somebody is screwing up, then it's up to you to get on his butt. And remember what Father Hesburgh told you today."

Nothing was conceded in the first twenty minutes, as Notre Dame rushed ahead to a 47–33 lead, which included a twelve-point unanswered spurt with seven minutes gone in the half, and a seven-point spurt later on. Father Hesburgh's presence on the bench with the team seemed to set the players on fire. San Francisco once closed the margin to seven points, but the confident and poised Irish maintained their composure for a 78–66 victory. Tracy Jackson bettered his previous career game-scoring mark by a point as he chipped in for twenty-three points, while the starting five and John Paxson accounted for most of the playing time. Tripucka racked up twenty points and Woolridge grabbed nine rebounds, slacking off a little in the scoring department. But that was all right with Digger: Orlando was playing his rebounding role.

It had been a significant pair of games, even with the loss to North Carolina State. Although the team had split its "simulated NCAA weekend," a direction and attitude had emerged. Tracy Jackson summed it up best after the San Francisco game. "We looked at this as a special game, we wanted it to be a turning point for us," he told the press contingent. "We wanted it badly, we wanted to start a drive toward the playoffs. We had a team meeting. We discussed the things we were doing wrong and brought everything out on the table. We were very open and admitted our faults with everyone having his say. We needed to keep the team's unity and there was a hunger to win this game."

There were only a half-dozen games left in the Irish season; now it was time to keep that attitude going.

13
THE IRISH ROAD SHOW

New York City holds quite a few memories for Digger Phelps. He began his head coaching career at Fordham, beat Notre Dame as coach of the Rams in that first season, and then, years later, turned down an opportunity to begin a new coaching career with the New York Knicks. Now he was returning to the Big Apple to showcase the Notre Dame program as the main event of a Madison Square Garden twin bill. Unlike the San Francisco, Tulane, or Texas Christian games, the Fordham contest was the homecoming for the team's head coach. And it almost wasn't a very happy return, either.

After leading Fordham to an amazing 26–3 record in 1970–71, his first reign as a head coach, Digger had taken the Rams to a third-place finish in the NCAA's Eastern Regional. That resurgence of a squad that could claim only a mediocre 10–15 season mark the year before Digger came on the scene earned shiny laurels for the new coach. The Metropolitan Basketball Writers Association awarded Digger its Coach of the Year honor while the United Press International poll listed Digger fourth on its own Coach of the Year list—recognition some coaches never receive in a career, let alone during their initial taste of authority. But New York basketball fans received only a brief taste of Digger's magic when the twenty-nine–year–old Fordham pilot left for the job he dreamed of: the head coaching role at Notre Dame. To this day some Fordham fans won't forgive Digger for what they feel was an abandonment of their program. But for Digger the Irish coaching position was what he had been working for in seven years as a graduate assistant, high school, and freshman coach. And that feeling hadn't changed when Digger declined Sonny Werblin's offer of the Knicks coaching spot. Notre Dame was perfect for Digger and he was perfect for Notre Dame.

But now it looked as if Notre Dame was the perfect opponent for Fordham on February 14. The first half of the game was an

122

atrocious exhibition of basketball by the Irish, who could only struggle along, turning the ball over to Fordham ten times and missing fifteen attempts while converting on thirteen field goal tries. Fordham and Madison Square Garden sensed a major upset as Irish players were strapped with fourteen personal fouls, including three apiece for Woolridge and Tripucka. Coach Tom Penders's players responded by sinking fifteen of eighteen free-throw attempts and Fordham led Notre Dame, 37–29.

Digger was burning when he headed for the locker room at the intermission, ignoring some well-wishers as he prepared his halftime comments. They were brief. "You guys are sitting here in Notre Dame uniforms," he yelled, "and you're spoiled—because you didn't have to work to build the reputation that uniform stands for. You weren't here when we went six and twenty, when we were humiliated by UCLA and Indiana. Now we trail Fordham by eight points because we were cocky and expected them to roll over for us because we're Notre Dame." That was all. It was enough. Notre Dame came back to take the game by 86–76.

Back in the locker room Digger was hoarse from shouting instructions to his team over the din of the Garden crowd. But he could still talk, and he was glad to. "We're playing to win now," he said. "Tonight we learned about being mentally ready to play. It's not easy to put yourself in a hole and get out of it, but tonight we did that. In Philadelphia we didn't respond to the pressure—in New York we did."

Now he spoke of the South Carolina game, two days off. This one had a special significance for him. Frank McGuire, South Carolina's coach, had always been one of Digger's favorites in basketball; he symbolized class and propriety in the coaching ranks, as did Ray Meyer of DePaul. But now McGuire was being forced to resign by the school's officials, and Digger didn't like it. "Twelve thousand fans will be rooting for Frank and those same fans want him fired," he told his players. "South Carolina will play for the moment and we'll be ten points down at the start of the game as far as I am concerned. Remember that in the next few days and think about starting right from the beginning with the intensity you played with here in the second half tonight."

It was now eleven-thirty and by the time everyone dressed and showered it would be midnight. But Digger decided to reward the players with a night on New York City instead of setting a curfew and checking their hotel rooms. "You guys earned it tonight," he said, "so go ahead out on the town, have a few beers and get something to eat. But don't go out and get sauced; you have nothing to prove. You're men and I'm going to treat you like men. If you get to bed by two or three o'clock you'll still get seven or eight hours' sleep—don't neglect your rest.

"And don't forget, South Carolina will be a pit and we're pointing toward a title we can't let slip away. You're representing Notre Dame and most importantly, yourselves. Think about that while you have a good time."

The game would be played at the Frank McGuire Arena of the Columbia Coliseum; but the proud, distinctive feeling McGuire had felt when the arena was named in his honor was now hollow after the controversy that encircled the Gamecock team last fall. South Carolina's elder statesman of basketball had been pressured to retire by the school's athletic board and the result was a disjointed season for the players. The Notre Dame–South Carolina game would be McGuire's retirement testimonial, and Digger feared the emotional lift the Gamecocks would have in their favor.

"Today I want to see everyone pumping each other up," he said, "whether it's on the court or on the bench." He also warned against a weakness that had been very apparent in the Fordham game: "Everyone comes after us at the beginning of the game because we let them." And finally, he called for a transition game that afternoon, hoping the running style would wear down the weaker opponent.

After Digger had presented McGuire with a monogrammed Notre Dame blanket as a retirement gift just before the tip-off, two words—"deliberate" and "awesome"—summed up the Irish effort. The players charged ahead, 38–21, as Tripucka and Woolridge continued their surge with fourteen and ten points respectively. South Carolina just couldn't keep up as Digger used his starting five for only the twelfth time in twenty-three games. In the end, Notre Dame scored almost at will as they whipped the ball around the court enroute to a 90-66 win. The box score read: Jackson 5 points; Tripucka 29 points; Woolridge 18 points; Branning 14 points. Only Bill Hanzlik failed to match the offensive output, with two points before fouling out. Digger's postgame comments were brief as he hurried to an interview with the NBC crew that had telecast the game regionally. Also in front of the cameras was Frank McGuire, who spoke generously about Digger's team. It was a sad way to end a distinguished career, but the gray-haired coach had only respect for his conquerors. "Tripucka was outstanding and Tracy Jackson is just great," he said. "They missed Tripucka when he was injured, but now that he's back and they're healthy the Irish can go a long way in the NCAA playoffs. Digger eased up a little in the end"—McGuire smiled wistfully— "he could have scored one hundred points." Digger was no less gracious, both in the television interview and later with the press, as he described the man he respected and the effects of the controversy surrounding him. "What went on affected this team emotionally," he said. "It's tough to pinpoint that psychological element but I have to feel it had a great impact on the players. Turmoil always leads to second-guessing." It was something he well knew from personal experience.

One of the game officials probably summed up the mood best when he remarked that Frank McGuire had more retirement gifts than wins that season. College basketball had lost one of its gentlemen.

Basketball statistics usually aren't worth the paper they're written on; a stats expert can usually manipulate numbers to prove whatever he wants. The only true number is, of course, the final score, something even the least knowledgeable observer can fully comprehend. Another obvious statistical statement is a player's offensive output; it glares from the box score with a summation of how well that man shot from the field and the free-throw line. Those numbers don't leave much room for interpretation and they can be used by broadcasters and newspaper writers as some measure of a player's abilities. Defensive abilities, however, aren't well defined because there are no clear-cut statistics in the box score. With rapidly changing defense alignments that often switch from man-to-man to zone configurations with each trip down the floor, it's usually impossible to have a clear idea of how well one player defended another team's player over the course of a forty-minute game. Thus, while defensive ability is often elusive in statistical terms, the Xavier game posed the perfect comparison of the worth of strong defense and easily measured offense.

The Musketeers' season had been a tough one: seven wins matched against fifteen losses for first-year coach Bob Staak. Yet, buried within their statistics sheet were four starters with double-figure scoring averages. Forward Jon Hanley averaged 18.2 points per game while Gary Mesa boasted a 15 point average. Center David Anderson was good for 12.5 points a game, and guard Anthony Hicks tossed in a 13.6 average. The rest of the club's statistics added up to 77.3 points, mean, per game while Notre Dame's team-scoring average was only three tenths of a point better entering the game. If the Irish scored that many points in each game they'd have lost only to Kentucky and posted a twenty-two–and–one mark. Tripucka (15.6 ppg), Jackson (14.7 ppg), Branning (12.5 ppg), and Woolridge (11.0 ppg) were the only four Irish players in double digits, and some of their performances couldn't match Xavier's individual efforts. But the Irish season record stood at seventeen wins and four losses, almost an exact flip-flop of the Musketeers' seven wins and fifteen losses. The difference was defense and it would be evident even in that night's game.

Digger began his talk to the team in a low-key manner as he prepared them for the Riverfront Coliseum contest. The team was dressed in blue-and-gold football warmup shirts, not to set new fashion trends but because some of their regular warmup garb had been stolen. Notre Dame Equipment Manager Gene O'Neil came up with the football attire and Digger decided to dress the entire team in the jerseys even though only a few players' jackets were missing: the team should look like a cohesive unit as well as play like one, and in fact the gridiron appearance he stumbled across was one that struck him favorably. The history of the Xavier game was comprised of physical contests and the football warmups might provide a twinge of intimidation during the pregame loosening routine.

"Xavier is a much better team than their record indicates," Digger cautioned as he laid out the game strategy. "Respect them tonight because it's the end of their season and they're looking for a big win to wind up the year. The keys tonight will be playing good defense and moving the ball against their zone for good percentage shots." It was now four games since his team had been humbled at home by North Carolina State and Digger was trying noticeably to avoid harsh tones to motivate the men. He would leave motivation to the co-captains and the players themselves; then, if they couldn't fire themselves up, he'd enter the picture.

And that was the case at halftime, when the Irish found themselves trailing Xavier, 36–32. The team had made only twelve of thirty-two shots from the field while Xavier clicked on fifteen of thirty-one attempts. The Musketeers' .484 shooting percentage, too, had soared well above Notre Dame's .375. So Digger now abandoned his quiet manner.

"You weren't ready to play tonight and you stunk," he said straight off. "You let them shoot and turned the ball over to them — you can't do that against a good shooting team." By now he was yelling again, as he reminded the team that it hadn't yet received an NCAA bid even though only four games were left on the schedule. If the team lost any of those games it would be putting the pressure on itself and the close of the season might seem more important than the NCAA tournament that would follow.

Then, suddenly, his voice softened: "Go out there in that second half and get into your rhythm. I don't want national headlines tomorrow spelling out an Xavier upset. They believe they can beat you now. Just play with pride—and play defense."

And the team lost no time surging ahead, 44–36, shooting the eyes out of the basket and leaving Xavier in a cloud of dust. Notre Dame only missed three baskets during the entire second half, in what Digger termed an "awesome display." Tripucka hit three baskets, Jackson seven field goals, Woolridge three, Branning seven, and Paxson a two-pointer. Only Varner, Andree, and Hanzlik missed one shot apiece en route to an 85–72 victory. The team showed patience on the offense while its defense held Xavier to five points below its own offensive average. It looked as if the Irish were coming on, and that the players were prospering by fewer substitutions. Digger realized that some of the men hadn't played as much as they'd have liked to, so after the game he spoke of the family concept and the commitment it would take to achieve the team's goal.

"It's tough sitting there on the bench," he said, "and I want you starters to forget about yourselves and help Stan, Mitch, Tim [Andree], and Bill [Varner] suck it up. I want the rest of you to pump them up, too. They're committed, too—they're making a contribution to the team. We're all a part of this family."

While the Irish had been busy with the Musketeers, a heavy fog had rolled into Cincinnati, cause enough for Digger to order buses for the trip back to South Bend instead of flying charter as originally planned. The Evansville disaster was etched in his mind as he remarked, "I'm not going to be fooling with your lives. We'll be busing back, so forget about the inconvenience and think about what we're accomplishing as a team. I don't want to pull another Evansville."

14

TAKE ONE STEP BACKWARDS

With twenty wins under its belt, the Notre Dame team suddenly took a giant step backward. They lost to Marquette's Warriors in a nationally televised afternoon game in South Bend, February 24. The teams seemed to be closing ranks and developing winning styles as the season wound down. But the unpredictable character of college athletes chose this moment to surface. The emotional highs and lows that are a part of dealing with teenagers and young adults materialized. The game disintegrated into a display of individual talent rather than a unified, disciplined team effort.

The Marquette series has had a special flavor of its own in Irish basketball history. The record books are dotted with great matchups like Austin Carr versus Dean Meminger, John Shumate against Maurice Lucas, Adrian Dantley lining up with Bo Ellis and—most recently—Bill Hanzlik blanketing Butch Lee. There have been other thrilling memories like the 96–95 double-overtime battle when the modern-day Irish–Warrior series resumed after eleven years with a Notre Dame victory in 1973. Like the Irish–UCLA series, Digger's charges ended a Warrior streak when Dwight Clay's monumental jumper from the corner with two seconds left put a halt to Marquette's eighty-one–game home-court record. And as recently as last season, Notre Dame staged one of its most dramatic comebacks in A.C.C. history. Trailing 39–25 at the half, the Irish erupted to outscore the visitors, 40–20, in the final twenty minutes, and thus defeating the number-one ranked Warriors. Bill Hanzlik emerged from that game with a reputation as one of the best defensive players in the country after stifling All-America guard Butch Lee, who only scored on six of nineteen attempts. In fact, the entire Marquette quintet played the last 4:39 of the game without scoring a single point until a final desperation shot at the buzzer.

Still, the Marquette game did not demand the same total commitment as the UCLA basketball rivalry or the USC football classic. It could be that an independent Catholic university from Milwaukee, the beer capital of the world, didn't engage or challenge the student body as a California school did. At Notre Dame a UCLA or Southern Cal week was like a crusade. Dormitories displayed banners while pep rallies and parties rocked the campus in anticipation of the big game. The mood for the Marquette game was zany, unexpected, and loose; much like the personality of Al McGuire, the former Warrior coach who had captured the spotlight in the series.

In 1976 Marquette had beaten the Irish at the A.C.C, 81–75, in one of the last games McGuire coached in the college ranks. The confident New Yorker was in the visitors' locker room, calmly shaving while his team warmed up in front of the Notre Dame student body. In a noisy ritual the student section showered the visitors with colored streamers when the Irish entered the arena before the tip-off; yet the unruffled McGuire chatted with visitors in the locker room, finished his grooming, and donned a bright red sports jacket while passing out a few "Al McGuire for President" buttons. With such a relaxed approach, McGuire inspired his team to victory; but it was the scene at the end of the game, when there was little doubt of the outcome, that best summarized the series' mood. McGuire played to the student body that had razzed him throughout the game for his bright attire. Like Moses leading a throng through the Red Sea, he raised his arms and turned to the students as if he could control them with his gestures of defiance. It was all the students needed to see. They roared their approval. A year later McGuire would answer a few good-natured hecklers at a basketball pep rally by remarking, "If you don't behave I'm going back to Marquette to start a football program." That was McGuire, witty, unpredictable, and irrepressible. Even in his absence the Marquette–Notre Dame series reflected his personality, but because the "Digger and Al Show" had been broken up like many a duo, Digger would have to solo this Sunday afternoon. He thought he had the jacket for the occasion.

It certainly was an attention-getter. Digger emerged from the locker room in a hot pink sport coat that he had picked out at Gilbert's Men's Shop, where he did most of his shopping. But if the jacket was outrageous, it had competition: Digger had complemented it with blue jeans and a pink shirt. Later he said, "I thought the pink coat would set up the game; it was wild and that's the type of afternoon I expected." NBC Commentator Dick Enberg was kind, referring to the coat as "strawberry colored." But if the video engineers in New York had been courtside, a tiny message might have crawled across the bottom portion of the screen reading "Don't touch your dial, the problem is not in your set." The jacket was pink and it did set the mood—before the contest. Afterwards, the color of the day would turn to fire-engine red, when Digger addressed his team following a humbling 77–74 loss.

The individual personalities of the players who characterized the past series carried over to the game. Sam Worthen took on an entire Irish team and won. The senior guard surpassed his season's best scoring effort as he singlehandedly dominated the game, scoring thirty points and inflicting foul trouble on whoever drew the task of guarding him. Three Irish players fouled out of the game, the most to leave a contest during the entire schedule. Oliver Lee also chipped in twenty points to help in the win, but in playing an entire forty minutes, it was "Sudden Sam" who bolstered his teammates' confidence following their embarrassing loss to Stetson four nights before. The Warriors also needed to win to boost them into the NCAA Tournament with their 15–8 record. Hank Raymond left South Bend with his sixteenth victory of the year and a bid tucked away in his pocket to be opened the next Sunday.

"Every guy took his own trip this afternoon," said an enraged Digger in a disheartened locker room after the game. "You weren't even in it from the beginning." But there wasn't too much time for recriminations. With De Paul, the undefeated number-one team visiting the A.C.C. in three days, Digger turned his attention toward that game, and stressed the need to learn from the Marquette defeat.

Earlier in the week De Paul sophomore sensation Mark Aguirre was quoted as saying Wagner College had a better chance of beating the Blue Demons than the Irish did. The remark caught as much attention as anything De Paul or its coaching staff had done during the season. Chicago wanted a winner badly and the city had adopted the college team. But Digger respected coach Ray Meyer, and wanted no ill feelings to arise from a player's remarks. He quickly set the stage for the confrontation with De Paul.

"You don't talk about De Paul—you just play them," he said. "If De Paul wants to talk about Notre Dame that's their business. On Wednesday we play the number-one team in the country and I don't want them laughing at you like Marquette is laughing now. You need fire Wednesday night because I've seen De Paul on television eight times and they're playing to perfection. They'll capitalize on your mistakes—something we don't do. They'll execute. Play a two-three zone—that'll force you to beat them."

The Marquette defeat was still stinging, but Digger continued to focus on the upcoming game. "We'll have two heavy practices this week and we will beat De Paul," he said. "You didn't have any fire today, but Wednesday we'll play with fire if I have to give you mine." He stabbed his chest with his index finger. Then he held out his hand and the team grouped around him. There was another figure taking part in the ritual, Jim Master of Fort Wayne. It wasn't the type of game the coaches liked a recruit to witness, but it was realistic and Phelps certainly didn't hold back any comments after the game on his account. Master's impression of the Irish and Phelps would be fresh now, unlike the one painted by other schools who were also recruiting the pure shooting guard. Each of the players placed his hand over Diggers. The psych for De Paul had already begun.

THE GIANT KILLERS

Few undefeated, number-one ranking teams come to play Notre Dame at the A.C.C. and leave with an unblemished record. Somehow, in some way, one miracle streak after another had been stopped on the Irish home court. Digger had made a career of pulling off major upsets, whether against UCLA, San Francisco, or Marquette. His Irish were, in fact, giant-killers. It was that knowledge that made the De Paul contest the most anticipated game on the Notre Dame schedule. As the college basketball season wound down, students and local townspeople began to root for Ray Meyer's Blue Demons to maintain their undefeated streak before coming to South Bend. Everyone felt that the Irish would beat De Paul somehow if the visitors came into the contest still undefeated and top ranked in the nation. And everyone wanted to be a part of the moment. Tickets were going for fifty dollars and some ingenious students had even taken to forging duplicates. One alumnus economics graduate student, Pete Harrington, flew back to South Bend for the game without even being assured of a ticket. He couldn't get one, but managed to sneak into the A.C.C. several hours before the tip-off. And he wasn't the only one to do it. By game time, the aisles were invisible as an overflow crowd filled the arena. The turnstiles read 11,600, more than 250 people above capacity. Digger couldn't disappoint that crowd.

He knew he'd have focus on psychology to prepare his team for the disciplined Blue Demons. The defeat by Marquette had been a bitter pill for the coaching staff and the players, but tonight was a new game. It must be set apart from Sunday's loss—and from whatever else might distract the team or inhibit the confidence it would take to beat De Paul. Digger was seeking a deliberate, patient effort by his players and he decided on a musical presentation to get the point across.

The mood was completely different from that of the Marquette game. Phelps wore modest garb—the traditional blue wool blazer and gray slacks—as he stood before the team. Then the tape player quietly pumped out "Bounce, Rock, Skate, Roll" by Vaughn Mason and Crew. As the Irish players tapped their feet to the beat of the music, Digger started his own song-in-prose: a speech his assistants later termed one of his best ever.

"Pride, that's what makes Notre Dame," he began as the semicircle of players absorbed the beat. "This is the moment. Forget about the season. It's tonight. Forget about the playoffs, that's next week... it's tonight." He then went on to forewarn the team about De Paul's tendency to let down during one point of a game, usually early or late. "They're ripe, they know it—and they're scared," he told his men. "Sure, they'll show some confidence. They'll talk. But they're scared of playing here tonight. Don't let that fear leave them. Capitalize on that fear."

As the beat of the music reverberated off the locker-room walls, Digger got into the technical points of the game plan, the special offenses, and the diamond-and-one defense that he had planned specially for De Paul's sensational Mark Aguirre. The beat continued and Digger took it up—almost in a chant: "It's to the rhythm tonight, fellows...two by two by two....Poise...wait...strike when it's there. Nobody be*lieves* in us; they don't think we're that *good.* You and I know how good we *are*; that's *all* that matters."

Now there was a lull in the music, and Digger also paused, waiting for the final bars. Then he delivered his own coda, saying, "This is a national *championship* game. Not in Market Square, but right *here,* in *South Bend.*"

On that note the song ended. The team was loose and excited. Now it was time to get a playing rhythm to match the music.

While the team went through its shooting drills Digger stayed behind in the locker room. Well-wishers stopped in to bid him good luck, but one man was conspicuously absent. Sports Information Director Roger Valdiserri's father had died and Roger was home with his family. Roger was a close friend of Digger's; Digger had already made plans to fly to the funeral on Friday morning and then get back to South Bend in time for practice Friday afternoon. But now he had to think only of the De Paul game.

Showmanship has its own role in championship basketball, and the A.C.C. crowd had grown accustomed to Digger's act before a big game. He would emerge from the tunnel and walk to the corner of the court, pretending he couldn't hear the crowd yelling and screaming in preparation for the team's entrance. Now, under a battery of TV and press cameras, Digger first gestured with his hands at his waist, signaling for a louder response. The roar became deafening but Digger put his hands to his ears as if straining to hear. Finally, he turned and gestured to the team and the A.C.C. erupted with a sound explosion as streamers came down like a rainbow-hued deluge. Television cameras panned across a crowd that was dotted with bright-green derby hats—handed out for the game by the Tip-Off Club. It was enough to give a Notre Dame fan or alumnus that surge of nervous excitement and pride that accompanies those special Notre Dame sporting events ... that feeling of pride and exhilaration at the bottom of one's stomach that signals a special personal moment. Notre Dame exuberance had gone into high gear: the De Paul game was one of those moments when the Irish tradition came alive.

And for Rich Branning and Bill Hanzlik, the senior co-captains appearing before the A.C.C. crowd for the last time, it was an especially meaningful going-away party. As the starting line-ups were announced, Branning and Hanzlik embraced each other and then ran out onto the court on cue. Branning had been banged up in the Marquette game, suffering a minor knee sprain that could have sidelined a lesser player. But his pride and desire to play overcame pain and handicap alike. Digger knew that a lesser player might not have gone into the game, but Branning had been iron man throughout his career—and the doctors didn't think the sprain was serious enough to sideline him. Besides, De Paul's Jim Mitchem was also playing injured; he had broken his hand in a slip on an icy patch of sidewalk. Still, he'd start at center—bandaged up. Staying out of the game would figuratively have killed Branning.

When the game finally began Notre Dame jumped to a 12–4 lead, on three baskets by Kelly Tripucka and single markers by Tracy Jackson and Branning. Ray Meyer signaled for a time out when Rich's twenty-three–foot jumper ripped the cords. The Irish controlled the tempo, building a 28–21 lead, although it diminished to 32–31 at the half. It was everything the press had written and the fans expected. There were only a dozen turnovers for both teams combined, with seven going to the Irish—five of those to Branning and Hanzlik.

That was one of the areas Digger pointed out during halftime. He spoke quietly, feeling no need for harsh words or strong statements. Again he reminded the team to be patient, to pull the ball out and start a play over if the shot wasn't there; "make twenty passes if you have the lead and get a good shot." He also pointed out that De Paul wasn't responding well to a Notre Dame checking play, and drove home once more the value of tough defense. Tracy Jackson had three fouls, but Digger told him to play as if he had none. Then he concluded: "You've all played a helluva first half against a national-championship caliber team—let's keep it up another twenty minutes."

Actually, it would take another thirty minutes. The second half began with spurts by each team. De Paul ran off six in a row and then the Irish answered with nine straight of their own. The game seesawed back and forth until Jackson tied it up with just over a minute left in regulation. Each team had a chance at a winning basket. De Paul's Teddy Grubbs threw the ball out of bounds and Billy Hanzlik traveled on a layup with eight seconds left. As the crowd held its breath Clyde Bradshaw's twenty-three–foot jumper hit the back of the basket and bounced away. The paying customers and everyone else were going to be treated to at least another five minutes of basketball.

During that five-minute overtime the Blue Demons crept ahead, 70–68. De Paul had made a habit of winning tight games all season and now it looked as if they were about to do it again. But fate stepped in when Rich Branning pulled up for a jumper with seven seconds left—to send the game into a second overtime. Two and a half minutes remained when Bill Hanzlik tied things up, and then Orlando Woolridge sank two key free throws with nineteen seconds left. Mitchem and Bradshaw had one final shot apiece, but Orlando's margin stood. Once again, the Irish had stunned another undefeated, number-one-ranking team—and pandemonium broke loose at the buzzer.

The first thing Digger did was race to the De Paul bench and embrace Ray Meyer. Then he flashed a number-one signal with his hand to the student body and fought his way through the crowd to the locker room. The scene here was as wild as the one taking place on the A.C.C. hardcourt. Music blared as players stumbled into their usually serene inner sanctum. They didn't mind the intrusion. The starting five had logged at least forty-three minutes of play, with Tripucka and Woolridge reaching fofty-nine and forty-eight minutes respectively. Only Varner, Paxson, and Salinas had cracked the lineup, but that was the last thing on anyone's mind. The Irish family eked out a 76–74 win over the only undefeated major college basketball team in the nation. Digger was on top of one of the locker-room stools, swaying back and forth in a disco step and snapping his fingers to the beat while his players—arm in arm in a ring around him—sang the words to "Bounce, Rock, Skate, Roll," opening and closing the circle and kicking their legs out in unison. The party was on.

When things calmed down a little Digger assembled the team. "You guys are unbelievable when you want to be," he told them. Tom Hawkins was hoping to interview Digger on the Metro Network, but Digger declined and substituted Danny Nee. It would be good exposure for his senior assistant as he began looking for a head coaching position of his own. Digger now started to tell his players to enjoy the night when Billy Hanzlik interrupted with a yell: "We're going to win it! I know it!" The NCAA Tournament was on every player's mind, and every player was certain that the De Paul win would help Notre Dame into the top-seeding bracket. Digger said it all: "They'll believe nobody ever comes to Notre Dame undefeated and number one and leaves that way." The team burst into a cheer. "Be humble and praise them," he stated.

Then Digger said, "Remember fellows—it's staying to the beat."

16

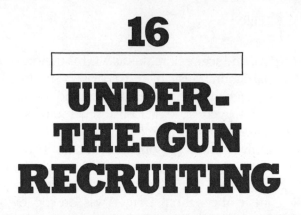

UNDER-THE-GUN RECRUITING

The dust on the A.C.C. hardcourt had barely settled before the coaching staff was facing up to another crucial strategy. The foursome would have to huddle and make some quick judgments about a recruiting plan that must be implemented in the next twenty-four hours. Harding High School coach Harlan Frick delivered word that Purdue coach Lee Rose had asked guard Jim Master to decide between Purdue and the other schools recruiting him by Sunday. Rose, a silver-haired Kentuckian, was forcing the high school senior into a difficult decision during preparations for the Indiana state high school tournament—more appropriately tagged as "Hoosier Hysteria" for the overwhelming interest Indiana always displays. The year before, Harding had captured the sectional and regional championship; and coach Frick couldn't help thinking that history might repeat itself. Frick had directed the recruiting visits of the college coaches, attempting to shield Jim, the Master family, and the Harding team from the distractions and bother that accompany high-level college recruiting.

The young head coach had shouldered the responsibility well; the college recruiters were treated equitably and aboveboard. After Lee Rose had used his last visit allowable under NCAA guidelines, Frick thought it only fair that Notre Dame and Kentucky should have the same opportunity to meet with Jim before the Sunday deadline. Kentucky's presence in the recruiting struggle had been more obvious in the beginning of the season, but more recently the Wildcats seemed a distant third. Joe B. Hall was in attendance at one of Master's games the weekend before; yet it appeared that the decision would boil down to Purdue and the Irish. The Sunday deadline disrupted all of Notre Dame's recruiting strategy, as Digger and Nee's approach had been low key all along.

On the opening night of the season Digger had encouraged Master to take his time in deciding between schools, advising that Notre Dame would wait for him as long as necessary. At this time, in fact, Digger was about to mail a letter to Master, outlining his role on the team if he chose Notre Dame for his college career. The letter promised no starting job; instead, it gave an honest evaluation of the returning nucleus and what it would take for Master to become an integral member of the 1980–81 Irish. But now Rose had called Digger's hand and the scramble was on.

Digger, Tommy, and Scott met in Digger's office to get the latest word from Danny Nee, who had just talked with Frick. The word wasn't good: "Purdue is putting the heat on," said Nee. Four days remained for Master to decide, and there were several problems and scheduling conflicts the coaches would have to work around. One was the Dayton game on Saturday afternoon, March 1, another was Digger's attendance at the funeral on Friday for Roger Valdiserri's father. These problems illustrated the kind of monster college recruiting had become. With Master viewed as a significant talent, it was a drop-everything situation when the status quo had been disrupted by Purdue. Drop almost everything, that is.

Danny Nee felt Digger should make his visit on Sunday and get the last shot at Master. If Digger went earlier, Nee feared Joe B. might react to whatever positive impressions Digger would make with Jim and twist them around to favor Kentucky. That wouldn't work, though, because Digger had promised Jim he'd be in attendance for the last game of the season. "I told him we'd keep our approach low key and that we'd wait for him to decide."

Nee, who was the chief recruiter, now offered an alternative plan: "We've got to map it out to him. I think his father wants him to stay in state, but the problem areas will be substitutions and the number of guards we have next year." Digger replied that anyone who saw the De Paul game should realize the substitution policy wasn't a factor, which brought Nee to the next concern. "The key is Tracy Jackson being moved to guard next year," he said. "I think Jim is afraid that he'll be the fifth guard coming in if Jackson gets switched to the back court."

The brainstorming continued, with Digger maintaining it would be better to visit Master at home the night after his final game. "I've got to go tomorrow because I promised him I'd be there," he said. "I've just got to explain that I'm using my second visit to tell him to wait and make a clear decision. I'm not worried about Kentucky, let's just be cool and aggressive."

Each recruiting effort was different, just as the player's personality. Notre Dame's new prize center, Joe Kleine, made an early commitment to avoid the onslaught of home-state support the University of Missouri would have burdened him with during his final high school season. Master was a different situation and the coaches needed a different approach. "I think we're tied if you looked at the overall picture," expressed Phelps. A few years ago the Irish were the leader as Master grew up in nearby Plymouth and dreamed of attending Notre Dame. "We're in a good position now; that's proved by the fact Purdue is panicking."

Still there was one consideration left in deciding on the day of Digger and Nee's visit. "What if he loses tomorrow night?" asked Nee. If Master lost his last game he might not be in much of a mood to talk. With the funeral on Friday as well as practice and a flight to Dayton for the Saturday game, the team commitments eliminated every day but Thursday and Sunday, and Digger ruled out Sunday. "Sunday is bid day and we have to man the phones and get geared up for the tournament," he said. There would be game plans, scouting assignments, travel schedules, and numerous other details.

"Besides," Digger added, "I don't like the double-barrel approach if Joe Hall comes in Sunday, too." Kentucky was involved with the Southeast Conference tournament and Digger speculated that Hall wouldn't have much time to get away before Sunday unless a booster provided a plane for a quick trip to Fort Wayne. "I don't like the idea of Jimmy being bombarded by two coaches in a matter of a few hours." As he spoke, his eye struck the letter on his desk; Dottie had typed it. "Rather than confuse Jim," concluded Digger, "we visit the family tomorrow night, give him the letter, and then leave him alone to think for a few days."

The decision had been made, and Digger now said, "Let's celebrate the De Paul game with a few beers at my house. Terry's back there with a crowd by now." Then he said, "Damn, I can't drink. I forgot I'd given it up for Lent." Danny Nee laughingly offered his own special dispensation. Digger also laughed as he declined, and the coaches repaired to his house—where the victory party was in full swing. Digger had missed a congratulatory phone call from his mother, in Beacon, New York, but everybody else was packed into the Phelps living room in South Bend: Jim Roemer, the dean of students, and his wife, Mary Ann; Vic and Bonnie McFadden; along with all the coaches and their wives. They all called for a comment from Digger, who rated the win as second only to the streak ending victory over UCLA in 1974.

And probably as amazing as the victory over the undefeated, number-one-ranking Blue Demons was the fact that Digger delivered his explanation with a glass of club soda in his hand.

National headlines greeted the coaches as they read the sports pages over their morning coffee. The CBS morning news segment ran a highlights clip and the Chicago media expressed shock that their beloved Demons had lost to the Irish. The overall implication was that De Paul had just had a bad night—one of those things that happens to any team. The Irish defense was barely considered a cause of De Paul's defeat—even though Ray Meyer had tried to put the press on the right track the night before, when he was asked why De Paul didn't get the ball to scoring sensation Mark Aguirre in the second overtime. "Notre Dame's defense," the grandfatherly coach had snapped back. "They played a fine, heads-up ball game. We have no excuses—we just lost it."

Meyer's words reflected his chief characteristic in thirty-seven years of coaching at De Paul: honesty. It was that quality that usually left rival coaches feeling guilty for beating him. Digger had felt that twinge of remorse when he embraced Ray after the game.

By six o'clock Thursday night the thrill still hadn't worn off in South Bend as Digger and Danny Nee prepared to drive to Fort Wayne for their visit with Jim Master. Digger wrapped himself in his heavy fur coat for the trip, but Nee suggested that a conservative blue topcoat would be more appropriate. Other schools have the habit of recruiting against Notre Dame by exploiting Digger's personality, interpreting it as flamboyant and egotistical. Nee suspected that that picture of Digger might have already been painted by one of the other schools recruiting Master; hence his recommending another coat. "You're probably right," said Digger, and retraced his steps back to the house. Digger is Digger, he is his own person and he doesn't compromise his individuality. He also happens to be a

clothes horse who enjoys fashionable attire. Yet, Digger knew Danny
was right about the coat and how even his choice of clothes might
be used to malign him. It seemed absurd, but the coaches had been
through it before.

En route to Fort Wayne, the two men talked happily about the
team and the win over De Paul. With a large cigar billowing smoke,
Digger was the picture of a proud father whose wife has just given
birth. But Fort Wayne was also discussed. Jim Master had attracted
more of Digger's attention than any other player he had ever
recruited.

Digger also mentioned recruits he had never seen in high
school, particularly Tom Sluby, a gem the Irish staff had just signed
to an institutional letter of intent. Sluby, a 6-foot-4 swingman from
Washington's Gonzaga High School, was a result of the efforts of
Frannie Collins, Notre Dame's Washington connection. Collins, a
retired vice-president of the Import-Export Bank, had become
involved with Irish basketball through former coach Johnny Dee.
Dee and Collins were old buddies from the Navy and Collins found
the recruiting chore like a hobby. His recruiting record includes
Austin Carr, Collis Jones, Sid Catlett, Chris Stevens, Adrian Dantley,
Duck Williams, and Tracy Jackson—and his efforts are priceless help
for the coaching staff. With Frannie handling the situation in
Washington by attending the high school games and reading the
situations, the coaches have only to follow his advice. And they
followed it well with Sluby.

"Sluby jumps like Orlando and can really jock some people
under the basket," said Nee, who had followed Collins's instructions
to the letter. Digger agreed: "He's a man playing a boy's game."

During the hour-and-a-half drive, Nee mentioned his own
recent interview for the Ohio University head coaching job the day
after the Xavier game. He didn't feel the interview had gone well,
but Digger advised him not to worry, pointing out that in four years
Nee had built a strong reputation. "You're in charge of recruiting
and people realize that we're still successful," he said. "Don't worry
about one job. I didn't get the Seton Hall or Dartmouth jobs when I
was looking around as an assistant at Penn." Soon the topic reverted
to the team and the psychological and physical readiness the
coaches felt entering the tournament. Digger had told the team to
go out after the game if they wanted and Danny questioned his

judgment. "You can't keep them in," replied Digger. "They went out last night and released all their frustrations. They're tired tonight and they'll get a good night's sleep," he judged.

Basketball talk was briefly interrupted by a news story on the car radio about the Ford Pinto trial that was going on in nearby Winamac, Indiana. Three teenage girls had burned to death when their 1973 Ford Pinto was rear-ended and then exploded in Elkhart County in 1978. Elkhart County Prosecutor Michael Cosentino had since brought precedent-setting criminal homicide charges against the Ford Motor Company. Digger had been following the trial closely; the product-liability aspect of the case interested him, as did Ford's chief defense attorney, former Watergate prosecutor Jim Neal. "I like Neal's style and confidence," he said. "He's like a gunslinger in the Old West; he hangs out in Winamac behind the scenes and manipulates the surroundings in his favor." Digger was far from indifferent to the families of the dead girls, but he calculated that time was on Jim Neal's side. "He'll probably pull it off because the country isn't ready for this type of consumerism. It's like smoking cigarettes—driving a Pinto isn't something you have to do. We're becoming a nation of small cars and it's up to a person to decide if he smokes, or if he drives a Pinto, or whatever."

As they neared Fort Wayne, the coaches briefed each other for their meeting with the Master family. Harding's coach Frick had told Nee, "Purdue is blowing your socks off," and Nee now prepared Digger for what to expect. "I'm not sure the kid likes you," he said. "He's probably been told 'Digger's the star—he overrecruits and he's stockpiling players.'"

Nee's predictions seemed valid when Digger met Jim after the game. Harding had trailed in the first quarter, but then pulled away from New Haven—much to Digger and Nee's relief. Master himself had broken the city scoring record with his first basket; that would help put the meeting in a positive light. But when Digger went up to Master after the game Jim didn't quite look him in the eye. As Digger and Nee headed for a teacher's lounge to sit down with the family, both turned to each other and said, simultaneously, "I don't like this." Clearly, Notre Dame was behind in the recruiting game. Clearly, Digger would have to go to work.

Family meetings were Digger's forte; he could talk honestly with the recruit and the parents about just what Notre Dame had to offer, not only athletically but academically. "Every school should be selling academics," he now told the Master family, "but how many schools can say that their players all graduate, and do it with majors like engineering, accounting, and finance?" Going to athletics, he touched on concern of Jim Master and his father: the amount of playing time Jim might expect—and the age-old rap that he, Digger, substituted too frequently. Digger rattled off playing times from recent box scores, and put the negatives Master had heard into clearer perspective. He also told Master's father: "Paul, your son is going to play more than anyone's telling him, and he'll get a good degree, too." It couldn't be any other way, he explained, with two starting guards graduating. Still, this was a big consideration in winning Jim over.

Digger next asked Jim about his feelings on whatever he'd heard about the Notre Dame team—and its coach. "I've watched the other guards and I think I can play," was Jim's reply. "What about me?" asked Digger. "Come on and say it." Master responded with questions about the playing time, referring to Digger's homecoming games when a player might be given more time before his family or hometown fans. He also mentioned the substitution policy. Digger defended that policy with the national schedule that allowed a player to visit professional basketball towns, be exposed to upwards of forty million homes on television, and in many cases become a household word. As for his "clockwork substitutions," Digger carefully explained the tough decisions he always had to make as a coach, referring particularly to the Marquette and De Paul games. "Stan Wilcox's family was out for both games," he said, "and Stan played three minutes against Marquette and none against De Paul." He would not promise Master a starting job—that would be unfair to the other members of the Irish squad. Instead he spoke of Kelly Tripucka waiting until mid-January his freshman year before starting. "It's also like John Paxson's situation," he went on. "Just be patient and show me in the first part of the season." Master thought Paxson was not playing as much as he should, but Digger felt the senior experience of Branning and Hanzlik couldn't be overlooked.

It was odd how Digger had to pitch the recruit; many athletes would come to play at Notre Dame on a moment's notice. Master was all but being begged to come to the university, and yet he was hesitating. Many people felt Digger never recruited in Indiana; but it wasn't that Phelps neglected the Hoosier state, just that he never had much success. Digger described the small-classroom atmosphere Master could enjoy at Notre Dame—along with the later benefits of national alumni organizations. "When Adrian Dantley was traded to Indiana," he said, "the first call he got was from Billy McGowan, the president of the Indianapolis alumni group there. Billy helped A.D. get a place to stay and really made him feel at home."

Digger wrapped it up by telling Master, "I'm a small part of the school. Don't go to a school just for a coach." Everything appeared to be going well, Paul Master said he wanted his son to stay in the state—and that would seemingly narrow the field to Notre Dame and Purdue. Jim's only reservation by this time was that the Irish players "don't take it seriously—they care more about having fun than bearing down." That had been used against the Irish before; it stemmed from a remark Digger had made a few years earlier, when the team was in St. Louis for the NCAA's Final Four. "I'm not going to lock them in their rooms when we're in New York or make them sing songs on the way to a game," he had said. "Some schools have won a national championship and gone through hell doing it. Those kids didn't enjoy it and I don't think that's right." Digger asked Master to compare the dedication of Paxson, Tripucka, and the rest of the players and judge the story in light of their attitudes. Jim Master agreed—the Irish were dedicated to winning a national championship. "You've just got to put a college basketball season in perspective," said Digger.

He left the Master family with the letter he had written, again mentioning his waiting approach, and apologizing for having to visit on the night of Jim's last home game. Digger knew he wouldn't like such a distraction himself, and he wanted Frick and the Master family to realize that he appreciated their predicament. With that, the coaches headed back for South Bend, hoping the talk had been fruitful. Only time would tell.

17

ONE LAST HURDLE

Dayton was the only obstacle in the way of the Irish before the NCAA Tournament, and the anticipation of the team and its coaches was growing. Speculation was rife, too. Sportscasters and coaches were already starting to guess at how the NCAA Selection Committee would align the teams; another favorite topic involved which regional Kentucky should be sent to, since the first and second rounds of the Mideast Regional would be played at Western Kentucky and the regional semi-finals and finals would be held in Lexington. In an NBC interview at Dayton, Digger made it clear that it would be unfair for the Wildcats to be placed in the Mideast; if Kentucky and the Irish wound up together in the Mideast, he said, it would be as bad as the "neutral" Freedom Hall site he himself was locked into every year. A little politicking wouldn't hurt before the selection committee announced its weekend's efforts.

Before the game, someone asked Digger which team was showing up today: the powerful, disciplined team that handed De Paul its first defeat of the year, or the sleepwalkers who had been humiliated by Marquette. Digger relayed the question to his players as they prepared for the game, urging the team to be ready from the start. Dayton's record was an unexciting thirteen and thirteen and Digger didn't want his team to react complacently, as they had to La Salle and Marquette. The Flyers had a history of beating Notre Dame at Dayton toward the end of the year. Phelps had lost to the Flyers in 1971–72, 1973–74, and 1977–78 at the Dayton Arena. He expected a tough game. "We want a running game where we go after them," he said. "When we get beaten by a La Salle or a Marquette we're not ready and we don't get rebounding. Then, we sulk for a few days and wonder what we'll do the next game. Our goal is to be twenty-two and five so that we don't have to play the first round of the NCAA tourney Thursday night. Don't finish the season with a defeat; we've had enough stinking defeats, and by now we ought to know what we can learn from those."

After a short pregame chat with Flyer coach Mickey Donoher, everything seemed rosy to Digger—until it came time for Notre Dame to take its first round of warmups, about forty minutes before the tip-off. While Irish players took shooting practice they spent most of their time dodging toilet paper that was streaming down around them. They mentioned it to Digger when they returned to the locker room, but no one really took it too seriously. After all, visiting teams at the A.C.C. were showered with streamers and toilet paper when they first took the floor and turn-about was fair play. When the Irish team returned to the court for some final limbering up, the toilet paper barrage continued until the players went back to the locker for their final instructions. Then, as Digger and the team came through the runway, yet more toilet paper filled the visitor's half of the court. Digger delayed his entrance, remarking to Danny Nee that he wasn't going out for the introductions until he had to; there was no sense in playing sitting duck longer than necessary. Even during introductions, the tissue paper and oranges flew toward the bench. Even when the game began, the shower did not let up.

The last thing Kelly Tripucka needed was another injury, especially on the eve of the long awaited tournament. But in the first half Kelly was decked under the boards. As Digger and Trainer Skip Meyer hastened to his side a roll of toilet paper landed only a few feet from him. Digger scooped the roll from the floor and carried it to the scoring table and Donoher. Although he wasn't happy with the situation, his manner was calm as he asked Donoher to do something about the crowd. Donoher was a friend of Digger's; some years back, when things weren't going well at Dayton, Digger had gone to bat for Donoher at a booster club luncheon. The next day Dayton worked its magic against the Irish, beating the 1972–73 team and winding up with an NCAA Tournament invitation. A year later, when a group of Notre Dame students posted a "Dump Donoher" poster behind one of the baskets, Digger quickly had the sign removed. (Later he learned that some Dayton fans had put the students up to displaying the poster.) Now, Digger decided to call in the favors and ask Donoher to do something about the crowd. He didn't figure on Donoher's reaction.

"What do you want me to do?" he asked, to which Digger simply replied, "Make an announcement." Donoher said he couldn't do that, then shrugged and walked away toward the bench. At that point Digger began to lose his cool: after all, an announcement about throwing toilet paper at injured visiting players wasn't too much to ask. "Thanks, Mickey," he remarked. "Ask me to do you another favor sometime." It struck home. Donoher whirled and went for Digger, but was finally restrained by his assistants. Tripucka was taken out of the game, only to return a few minutes later. Fortunately Kelly was all right; his services would be needed if the Irish were to escape with their twenty-second victory.

With the contest tied, 32–32 at halftime, Digger's manner was cool and restrained. He remembered the Xavier contest and how his players exploded in the final twenty minutes. The team hadn't played that badly and his words, "Just play, fellows—we're okay so just stay with it," summed his feelings up. "I like the tempo of the game," he said. "We're controlling it. And then when we go ahead, we'll go zone and really tighten up defensively."

Also during halftime, while the Irish sat in their locker room, the Dayton vice-president, Tom Ferricks, announced a plea to end the toilet paper barrage in the second half. He was greeted with more toilet paper. Later, he apologized to Digger, explaining that a nearby bar opened at 9A.M. on game days and offered students all they could drink for two dollars. Digger readily understood the problem and accepted the apology.

When the Irish spurt came, nearby Kettering, Ohio, native John Paxson led the charge with five minutes remaining. The 50–50 score grew to 60–50 while Dayton was held scoreless until only 32 seconds were left. The final margin was 62–54 and the Irish were set for the tournament with a 22–5 record. Digger gave the players two days off to rest, relax, and hit the books. "Sacrifice tonight when you get back to campus," he said. "Don't party. Don't do anything that's going to distract you." Only seven players were to see action again, and Digger said that he knew it was tough. "I won't deny it. But just remember that it's tournament time now and it's up for grabs. If we win, it will be worth the effort."

Digger also prepared the team for any possible media confrontations, instructing the players how to react to the toilet-paper scuffle in the arena. "If anybody asks, just say it's one of those things and don't worry about me," he said. "Just show class and remember you're Notre Dame men."

NCAA Tournament time had finally arrived.

18

LIVING
FOR A
MOMENT

It was Sunday afternoon, March 2, but unlike other weekends the light was on in the athletic director's office. The NCAA bids were expected to be extended at two o'clock and Notre Dame officials huddled around the phone, speculating on where they'd be shipped for the regional.

Athletic Director Ed "Moose" Krause was off on a winter fishing trip in Panama and his assistant, Colonel Jack Stephens, was filling in next to the phone. Business Manager Joe O'Brien, Ticket Manager Mike Busick, and Assistant Sports Information Director John Heisler were also there in anticipation of the bid—and the work they'd be doing to organize an NCAA trip. While Colonel Stephens sat in the outer office the phone rang once and then twice. Impatiently, Digger yelled, "The phone, Jack. Answer the phone." Finally Joe O'Brien picked up the hot potato as Stephens reentered the room. Big Ten Commissioner Wayne Duke, who had chaired the selection committee, was on the other end. "The winner of the Missouri–San Jose game at Lincoln," repeated Stephens as Digger's face twisted into a grimace. The Irish were in the Midwest Regional, seeded fourth in that bracket along with LSU (24–4), North Carolina (21–7), and Louisville (28–3). It was a tough bracket, one of the two toughest, in Digger's estimation. Later, as the pairings were all announced, the coaches couldn't believe the Eastern bracket, with Syracuse (25–3), North Carolina State (20–7), Georgetown (24–5), and Maryland (23–6). "Tell me there's not any politics involved in this selection process," challenged Digger. "But at least we know where we stand. Now we've got to work our butts off."

Digger also felt that the Big Ten made out well in the bracketing. Purdue (18–9) and Indiana (20–7) stayed in the Mideast with the Boilermakers playing at home against La Salle (21–8) and then most likely Big Ten champion Indiana in the second round. Number-one ranking De Paul (26–1) was shipped out to the Western Regional with Ohio State (20–7), Brigham Young (24–4), and Oregon State (26–3). Barring a major upset a Big Ten school would make the Final Four, a financially rewarding position for the conference to be in if it worked out that way.

Digger's assistants now lost no time combing through the NCAA booklets that Phelps had made up the previous year, breaking down each coach's responsibilities. Tommy McLaughlin was already checking the videotape and film library that had been amassed over the season—by swapping with other schools or relying on an alumnus or friend to do the recording on his home videotape desk. Scouting had become scientific and with networks like ESPN doing more and more television broadcasts, a videotape recorder had become as necessary as a blackboard. The taped broadcasts paid off for the staff by reducing scouting trips—and costs.

The assignments were neatly broken down. In his six previous NCAA appearances Digger had developed quite a system for dividing the tournament duties. Danny Nee handled tickets, Tommy took care of scouting, and Scotty managed recruiting. All the details were covered—locker-room control and signs, bed checks, policing the floor the night before games, plugging the phones so that players' sleep couldn't be interrupted by overzealous fans of Irish opponents. All the media contact would go through Roger Valdiserri's office, while Tommy and Danny would oversee travel, practice, hotel, administration, and locker-room and equipment control. And if the Irish made it very far in the regional a command post would be organized with a member of the coaching staff manning it through the waking hours. The team would operate from the CP—the largest room the managers could find—where coaches could show films, hold team meetings, and even have team mass and meals.

Digger also set the mood for the week with some plainspoken words for his assistants about overreacting to his own verbal outbursts during the week ahead. He had been mild with the team throughout the year, but the assistants had often felt his wrath as he demanded their total attention. When Digger became wrapped up in a game, a practice, or even a scouting situation his striving for perfection didn't tolerate any mistakes. His assistants certainly realized that at the end of a season. "Let's get one thing straight," he said; "you guys have got to learn that when I get hot and start screaming and yelling at you, you've got to put it in one ear and out the other. I'm handling it with the team, but I don't want you guys getting hung up over my screaming. I expect it from the team, but not from adults. Danny, Kuchen, DiBiaso, and Frank McLaughlin have all learned to deal with it, but in situations where you don't learn from a mistake you deserve to get your butts ripped and I'll rip them. I don't have time for this nickel-dime stuff, so let it go in one ear and out the other."

After that, Digger and the coaches watched a Missouri–Kansas State tape and plotted their game strategy for the remainder of the afternoon. Then Digger headed for his hideaway on Lake Michigan for the rest of Sunday and Monday, to organize his thoughts for the tournament. Built by Knute Rockne, the house was a marvelous structure concealed in a wooded lot. Digger used the place to unwind and escape from the South Bend scene. Maybe he was counting on a little inspiration from the home's original owner, too.

On returning from the lakefront retreat, there was a good-luck message from attorney Jim Neal, together with one of the enormous cigars the lawyer was notorious for smoking. The cigars were so long and thick that they were almost visible before Neal could be seen coming around a corner. The note from the former Watergate prosecutor said, "I always admire Notre Dame teams for their class."

The preparations went just as planned when the Irish assembled to prepare for their first-round opponent. They'd face either San Jose or Missouri and the coaches were banking on Missouri to win. The players seemed rested from their two-day vacation from basketball, which was exactly what Digger had wanted when he gave them the time off; he couldn't see practicing all week for a Saturday game, peaking on Thursday afternoon, and coming out flat when it counted. All season he had pulled the team in and out of basketball situations, giving them a day or two of rest sandwiched between big games or tiring road trips. He himself welcomed a certain amount of time away from the basketball court, and what was good for him was good for the players.

The day before the game the coaches attended a press luncheon. As expected, Missouri had won the Thursday night game,

March 6, and coach Norm Stewart was in attendance along with
Digger. Usually the setting was a good place for reporters to get a
few quotes, but that day it was a sportswriter's delight. Stewart got off
a verbal attack on Notre Dame, criticizing the university and the
basketball program. The remarks were no doubt the result of a
recruiting battle in which he and Digger had locked horns over the
previous two seasons. Both coaches were chasing Steve Stepanovich, a center from St. Louis, Missouri, who was now playing
regularly for the Tigers. Stewart had thus won round one, but
Digger evened the match by signing Joe Kleine from Slater, Missouri, before the college season barely got off the ground. Kleine
had received at least fifty letters from Missouri politicians and
businessmen, urging him to remain in the "Show Me" state for his
college career—to no avail. So now, Stewart's remarks were bitter;
obviously turn-about was not fair play in his book. No pregame
pleasantries were exchanged before the game between Stewart and
Phelps.

   In the locker room of the Bob Devaney Sports Center, Digger
decided to continue his musical pep talks, exploiting the De Paul-
game theme song, "Bounce, Rock, Skate, Roll." He alluded to the De
Paul game, and the loss at Market Square Arena the year before to
Michigan State in the tournament. "You wouldn't think a year could
go this fast, but it has," he said to the players. "This is another one of
those special moments—and it will take five such moments to earn
a national championship." The music rolled on and so did Digger, as
he directed the team's attention to beating Missouri and forgetting
about other distractions like Stewart's verbal shots and the hostile
crowd.

   "Not many people believe we can win," said Digger, "but that's
fine because the pressures are on the other teams. When we go out
that door we'll leave this locker room as a family; if we don't worry
about beating Missouri no one else will do it for us. Today has
nothing to do with fans; we're the only ones who can win a national
championship. There have been some great things you've witnessed
in your young lives in sport, but what you can have in three
weekends is better than any part of it. We've tasted a little of it by
beating De Paul. Now go out and do the little things that will do the
big things for us." Digger was almost rolling with the music, talking
about the spurt the team had capitalized on against Dayton, and how

the same spurt would beat Missouri. "It's keeping it to the rhythm," he said, as the lyrics echoed, "It's disco time...ain't no stopping, keep on rocking...."

Then the music ended, and Digger turned to the blackboard where a simple game plan was drawn in chalk.

1. POISE AND PATIENCE
2. CONTROL OFFENSIVE AND DEFENSIVE REBOUNDING
3. SMART EXECUTION

"This game will be like a fifteen-round prize fight," said Digger. "They'll struggle, scrap, and stay close for twelve rounds. You'll win it in the last three. They'll try to win on guts and there's only one way to beat that—play with guts yourself." Digger knew his team was more talented than Missouri if the right team had showed up in Lincoln that day. "This is the first step back to Market Square Arena."

Digger was correct in his prediction about the struggle the game would turn into. The Irish led by six points at the half, 42–36. But Notre Dame had played so badly that Digger almost feared the team was asleep. "Every situation developed a breakdown and we beat ourselves," he told the players. "We're up by six points and we should be up by sixteen. "You can't relax against a club like this. If Tracy didn't keep us in the game with his offensive rebounding we'd be losing now." Angrily, he scanned the room, putting down the excuses he heard for one thing or another that had gone wrong. "They're playing on guts and we're playing on alibis. Every guy has an excuse for a bad shot or a foul and that's just how we lost to Michigan State last year. We beat ourselves the same way....

"Fellows, I'm trying to scare you into realizing you can lose a game the way you played in the first half. It's that close to being a blowout. In twenty minutes we can win and be on our way to Houston for the second step. Don't let it slip away."

It seemed as if the team was waiting for the spurt that never came; Missouri stayed with Notre Dame long past the twelfth round, capitalizing on the half-hearted Irish defensive effort. The Tigers came within an ace of winning the game in regulation, only to see Tripucka feed Woolridge a layup with four seconds left. But in overtime Missouri built an 84–80 lead and then got the winning point from once-recruited Stepanovich when he stepped to the foul line after Hanzlik fouled him with fourteen seconds remaining. The two teams swapped baskets amid time outs as Digger calmly encouraged his team that they could still win it. But as the Irish trailed by three points, 87–84, time ran out, and so did the season.

The locker room scene was like a funeral. Digger asked one of the managers to lock the door. His comments would be honest, without sugar coating, but without anger either. "They beat you with enthusiasm," he said quietly. "They're not a better team. We weren't in it mentally and although we could say we tried our best, I for one can't accept that. We didn't make it and for the guys who sat on the bench and felt they could do a better job, I'm sorry. I made the decision and I'll live with it.

"For our three seniors, you've given us four great years and I'm sorry we didn't win a national championship for you to go out on. You're three super guys who've been a part of our lives for four years; we'll need you for the next forty years, too.

"For those of you coming back, we have a long way to go next October. Today we got beat early and at the end of the game on defense, we had enough points to win. Remember, in life, when you need to gamble you can get burned. And when there's no need to gamble, I advise you—don't do it, especially when you have the lead. For the eight guys who played it just wasn't enough; Missouri beat you on guts and we stunk. When we come back in the fall and work on basics like flash pivots and back-door defense, remember this feeling today."

Digger then reminded the players of the basketball banquet set for the next week, and told them to be real Notre Dame men in defeat. As he huddled the team for the last time of the season his words were brief: "Remember we still have tomorrow, but we just let *now* get by us."

For the next few days Digger reflected on the team and the season. He spent Saturday night across the street with the McFaddens, looking back at the game over a few beers. The family was like a second set of parents for Karen, Rick, and Jennifer when Digger or Terry needed a babysitter. Digger needed a peaceful few days with friends, and the next day he and the family spent time with Jim and MaryAnn Roemer before going out for pizza and strolling through the Baugo Creek Nature Preserve. By Sunday night Digger was just plain grubby as he returned home with his family to watch a *Sixty Minutes* feature on Indiana's Bobby Knight. Digger had neglected to shave and his hair was matted down from the cowboy hat he'd worn at Baugo Creek. He was struggling to accept defeat for another year. For the next few days it would mean eating humble pie. (One of the toughest ordeals faced one freshman loser. John Paxson had said he didn't want to return to his dorm to face his fellow students after the Missouri game. Paxson was learning the lesson that defeat in basketball or business wasn't easy to accept; everyone likes a winner but nobody likes a loser.) Terry also knew there'd be some hushed conversations for the next few days while the loss was fresh in people's minds. As soon as the basketball season was over the Phelpses would slip out of town to leave it all behind for a while. After the banquet Digger's schedule of appearances and recruiting trips would begin again, but first he needed a vacation from basketball to reconcile the season's goal with the end result.

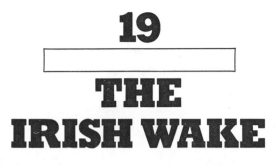

19

THE IRISH WAKE

The Notre Dame basketball banquet usually falls between a victory in the first weekend of the tournament and the regional semifinals; but this year the Irish had lost their first tournament game, also a first for Digger's Irish. In past years it had been easy to stand up in the A.C.C. basketball arena, which was now packed with tables seating local basketball fans, businessmen, and university officials. The talk usually drifted onward to the next tournament game, with promises of great things to come mixed with comments, by players and coaches, about the past season and the support of the Irish fans. This year would be difficult; the Notre Dame season had ended a mere forty-eight hours ago and it would take a big swallow of pride and disappointment to put up a happy front. Forty-eight hours wasn't much time to reconcile a season's dream and an unexpected wipeout of the team's goal. Still, as the old cliché has it, the show must go on. And when it finally ended the dinner crowd was on its feet, cheering the basketball team for its character, if not for its court performances. "I'm not going to dwell on the Missouri game," said Athletic Director Moose Krause. "I'm not ashamed of the record of our team. In the last five years we've won over twenty games a season and gone to the NCAA's. We're very proud of that effort by our players and our coaches." Krause wrapped it up by reminding the returning players: "We've got next year." Moose was a Notre Dame legend who attended as many Irish sporting events as the day allowed, scurrying from swimming to soccer, fencing to wrestling, baseball to tennis. He was a regular at basketball, football, and hockey games, easily recognizable by the cowboy hat always perched atop his head as a reminder of the football team's 1978 Cotton Bowl victory over Texas that earned the school another national championship. Krause loved athletics, he was the school's

last three-sport letterman until Bob Golic repeated the feat in
football, wrestling, and track. He never failed to realize the importance of the less glamorous Notre Dame sports and his presence at a
game once or twice a season was an inspiration to the student-
athletes.

Another figure in Notre Dame's athletic scene at the head
table was the Reverend Edmund P. Joyce, who talked about being
realistic in the sporting arena, knowing there would be losses when
they were least expected or wanted, and dismissing the team's
disappointment by bringing out the high points of the year. As a
leader in the university athletic structure, Father Joyce was not
concerned with winning at any cost. His philosophy—and Father
Hesburgh's—was to field a competitive athletic team to represent
Notre Dame while maintaining high academic standards. A coach
did not fear for his job after missing a national crown. As long as the
athletic program was competitive and did not embarrass Notre
Dame away from the playing field, the University was pleased and
proud.

"The mere achievement of being in the top ten in this nation
in a highly competitive sport that begins with hundreds, if not
thousands of good teams, is something we can be very proud of,"
said Father Joyce. "To have a record of twenty-two victories against
five losses during the regular season is nothing to be sneezed at;
there are very few teams in the country that have a record that good."
Father Joyce also pointed to the school's seventh consecutive NCAA
appearance and the giant-killer performance against De Paul.
"There are any number of reasons why I and the entire Notre Dame
community take such pride in this team," he continued, "and I
would say it's largely because of the type of young men that
represent us on the basketball court."

Then Digger spoke. He began by thanking the managers,
assistants, and other people behind the scenes. He also mentioned
the cheerleaders and their enthusiastic support through the season,
and jokingly remarked that "If Kelly had played defense the way he
followed the cheerleaders around, we would have won last weekend." On a more serious note, he spoke of the disappointing
season's end for his seniors. The letter "M" had been significant in
their careers, he noted, as he told of Hanzlik and Branning's first
game, an overtime victory against Maryland, and their final game, a

loss to Missouri. "Life is happiness to sadness; we teach it well at Notre Dame," he noted. "M" also stood for special *m*oments and *m*emories—and learning to peak for those moments and work through them not only at college but in life. "M" represented momentum, too: the Irish had it when they beat De Paul and Dayton. And of course, he said, " 'M' for Mary, Our Lady, Notre Dame." Digger paused briefly, then concluded. "To understand is to be sorry," he said. "Tomorrow's coming; we let *now* go by."

It had been hard for Digger even to speak; his team's performance, after all, had been the worst since his first season at Notre Dame. Standing back, one could see the dominant and successful program he had built when a loss in the first game of the NCAA Tournament was his second worst season. But toastmaster Jack Lloyd put it all in perspective, something he had a knack for doing. "It's pretty easy to give plaudits to the team for a great season with the knowledge we're going to move forward after already having won the first game," he said. "I hope you can all appreciate what this man has gone through in the last forty-eight hours, to stand up here before you this evening and talk about another great group of young men with the knowledge that they aren't going to go forward. All I can say, Richard, is that I've been with you as a winner and I've got to tell you that as far as I'm concerned this is your finest performance thus far at Notre Dame." From the applause that followed, one could see that everyone shared Lloyd's feelings.

Now the affair became less somber as Lloyd introduced the athletes. This was the guests' opportunity, he said, to see how the players conducted themselves in public. It had been decided the players should hand out the awards to their teammates—there was no need for an outsider to address a Notre Dame following. Not that past banquet speakers like Howard Cosell, Red Auerbach, and Abe Lemons hadn't been well received; it was just that the chemistry of this team was unique and it would be hard for someone else outside that basketball family to convey it.

And the players took the spotlight in a spirit of fun, talking about their resemblances to comic figures: Tim Andree to Jethro of the Beverly Hillbillies; the big-eared Stan Wilcox to Dumbo the Elephant; Kelly Tripucka as the team's "Ronald McDonald Award" recipient for his hairstyle. Graduating walk-on Tim Healy was dubbed Barney Rubble, while co-captains Branning and Hanzlik were tagged Woody Woodpecker and Herman Munster. The ribbing underscored the friendship that had developed among the men, on and off the court.

And the joking went on as the awards—almost every player got one—were presented. Mike Mitchell said there really shouldn't be a Father Tom Brennan Free-Throw Shooting Award because no one on the team had reached the 80 percent shooting mark Digger asked for before every game; but Mitch gladly made the presentation to his roommate, Kelly Tripucka. Digger didn't escape, either. Marc Kelly, the California walk-on, said that everyone had told him to put the needle to his coach, but that he had decided not to. "After all," he asked, "how's a man who wears a pink suit on national television going to defend himself?"

But the biggest response came when the team's two co-captains spoke. Hanzlik and Branning also joked a little, but their humility and gratitude came forth most forcefully. Perhaps Branning left the strongest impression when he summed up his basketball career at Notre Dame, which included the rare distinction of being the first four-year starter since Kevin O'Shea, who had played from 1946 through 1950. The soft-spoken member of the Christian athletes left the crowd with a line of poetry:

> *Talent is God-given, be humble;*
> *Fame is man-given, be thankful.*
> *And concede the self-given, be careful.*

"Thank you, Notre Dame," he concluded.

It was hard for anyone leaving the arena to feel any disappointment over the loss to Missouri.

In the days that followed Digger and the coaches found it impossible to forget about college basketball for very long. The day after the banquet Danny Nee was selected as the new Ohio University basketball coach, an announcement that delighted Digger: that made four former Notre Dame assistants who had become head coaches across the country in five years; this spoke volumes about Digger's own ability to develop his subordinates.

Digger also had to monitor guard Jim Master's situation with other schools. This meant staying close to home; he did not want to be out of town if a problem developed. But just a week after the

Notre Dame banquet he might as well have been in Alaska. The high school senior gave Digger a bad jolt when he called to say he'd be attending Kentucky next fall. Just a few weeks before De Paul had thought Dick Beale would be attending their school in the fall, but Beale shocked the coaches and switched his decision to Kentucky. Now, Notre Dame was victimized as well by a puzzling change of heart. The night before, he had spoken with Master on the phone, asking, "I'm not going to lose you, am I?" Master replied, "No, I don't think so." But the next morning Digger's office phone rang. It was Master and he was crying.

"Coach, I'm going to Kentucky," he said.

Digger was stunned. If he was going to lose Master, he had thought, it would be to in-state rival Purdue. He hadn't put much effort into recruiting other guards, such as Glenn Rivers, figuring that the closeness of Fort Wayne and Jim's desire to attend Notre Dame as late as the previous fall would bring him to choose the Irish. But Master had decided he'd have a better chance of starting at Kentucky, despite the graduation of Hanzlik and Branning. The next day Digger received a letter from Mrs. Master:

Digger:

We want to thank you for all the time you spent with Jim. It was the toughest decision he will ever have to make. Was so hard for him, as you have taken a special place in his heart and will always stay there. He cried after talking to you. Said "Mom, he is a great person, was so nice to me. I hope he is always my friend." Couldn't remember anything you said to him, but said "I know it was nice."

Paul and I are happy to have had you touch our lives. We wish you and your terrific staff all the best. Can't see how you can replace Danny, as he is a super person, but know you'll find someone of the same character as you would not have any other kind on your staff.

Jim picked this card; says it best.

Best of luck to you, your staff and N.D., will be following you again next year.

Paul, Sandra, Jim Master

And now, with the recruiting of Jim Master suddenly over—the wrong way—the Irish were back in the market for an incoming guard.

In the days and weeks that followed the well-organized files Danny Nee had left behind withstood a fine-tooth combing in search of the right player and personality that would best fit into the existing nucleus. By the end of April the coaches were lucky enough to sign Barry Spencer, who had really come on since Digger and Nee had watched him before Christmas. Spencer got back in the groove as his senior year went along, leaving Scott Thompson to declare "his moves are NBA quality" by the end of the year. Spencer would play guard for the Irish, instead of forward as he had for Catholic Central, Detroit's Catholic League champion. At 6 feet 7 inches, his height might remind people of another tall guard who had come to Notre Dame as a forward, Bill Hanzlik. Spencer wound up his final season with a 24.5-point, thirteen-rebound average and received *Parade,* McDonald, *The Detroit News,* and *Detroit Free Press* distinction. He also played a guard position in the playoffs and post-season all-star games, the final selling point for the coaches.

Another addition, one day later, was Cecil Rucker, a 6-foot-8 forward from Mackin High School in Washington, D.C., who fell in love with Notre Dame during a late visit to the campus. Rucker fit right in with the team and immediately ruled out other schools seeking his talents. With previous alumni like Austin Carr and Duck Williams hailing from Mackin, the coaches realized it was best to offer the talented forward a grant-in-aid now; next year his ability and attitude might be hard to equal. In one season Salinas, Tripucka, Jackson, Woolridge, and Wilcox would be gone; Digger was already looking a year into the future. Rucker had averaged twenty-one points and thirteen rebounds, winding up his Mackin career with over 1,200 points. "He's the kind of player who can still grow and add some weight to that 6-foot-8, one hundred ninety-pound frame, too," said Digger.

While Digger was trying to scout his own new players, he also had to concern himself with another type of recruiting. A few weeks before, he had been named coordinator of women's varsity basketball at Notre Dame, a step the university had taken to keep in step with Title IX—and as a good-faith measure for Irish coeds. It was Digger's responsibility to direct the program's rise to Division I status, complete with scholarships and a full-time coach.

"The women's basketball program will be top flight, and I think we'll be able to catch up quickly with other programs," he had said. As he had built his basketball program with help from Ara Parseghian and the football team's success, so Digger hoped his men's program would help produce a successful offspring: "We're going to have the women's team travel with us when we fly charter and play double headers against schools with women's programs."

Digger enthusiastically embarked on finding a coach who was familiar with Division I A.I.A.W. (Association of Intercollegiate Athletics for Women) basketball, although he also interviewed Sharon Petro, Notre Dame's successful Division III women's coach and physical education instructor. In the end, he chose Mary Di Stanislao, the Northwestern coach who had performed wonders with the Wildcats while winning the Big Ten crown in consecutive years. "Sixteen years ago Notre Dame went to Northwestern for a football coach by the name of Ara Parseghian," Digger told the press as he publicly introduced his selection. "This time we're going back to Northwestern, for Mary D." Mary would have little problem adjusting to Notre Dame's athletic and academic standards with her knowledge of similar standards at Northwestern. And she soon came to know at first hand the scramble the Notre Dame men's coaches had gone through in recruiting over the previous month as she hastened to begin recruiting some female blue-chippers for her own team.

Placing the women's program under the direction of the men's basketball coach had been a novel idea, but few doubted that Digger would get the women's program on its feet and on its way to Division I-caliber play. It was just like 1971 all over again. But this time another Irish coach might have to suffer through the growing pains.

20

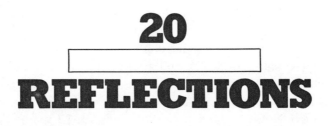

REFLECTIONS

The NCAA Championship night was as good a night as any for Digger Phelps to look back on the past season and talk about the direction college basketball was taking. UCLA—a team the Irish had beaten twice during the regular season—and Louisville were the focus of national attention on that Monday night, March 24. For NBC, the broadcast was also the network's opportunity to display its remote prowess, as Don Ohlmeyer and the NBC sports staff waited for official word on the United States' Olympic status. U.S. participation in the Moscow games was already in question, and judging from the way the broadcast was showcased, it appeared that the NCAA Championship game was just as special as a Super Bowl or the Olympics. College basketball was as marketable a sports product as any in the world; a few months later its professional counterpart would stage its own championship game with much less hoopla and with many television affiliates opting for a delayed tape broadcast after prime-time evening hours and local late-news shows—if the game aired at all in a market. There would be good reason for college basketball participants to be pleased with the popularity of the college game. No one realized this better than Digger, as he prepared to watch the contest with his family.

But he also knew of some unsavory particulars. Attention was now being heaped on what he considered mediocrity. Just as he had predicted in the fall, two unranked teams, in fact three, had survived the competition to meet in the Final Four. Iowa came out of the East with a regular season mark of 19–8; Purdue exploited its home-court advantage to travel to the semifinals after posting a similar 18–9 mark; and UCLA—with a 17–9 record—turned on in the tournament to reach the championship game. Only Louisville, standing 28–3, seemed to represent the cream of college basketball.

Digger felt that the optimal NCAA tourney configuration would find thirty-two teams distributed within four regions. "If you ran eight teams in each regional and played a double elimination tournament for two straight weekends you could have four winners who could go to the Final Four and have a great NCAA Tournament," he said. The playoff would resemble the college baseball world series, hardly an unspectacular alignment. However, Digger doubted that the arrangement would ever become a reality; there was too much political pressure from conference schools. "There's twenty-three teams that have to be invited as conference champions," he said, "despite the fact that a team with a losing record can win the conference tournament and gain an NCAA invitation. If the conference is that bad no one should be invited. But that will never happen."

It was not that Digger thought the arrangement would help his Irish; his seven consecutive appearances in the NCAA Tournament would rule out chalking his idea up to sour grapes. A double elimination playoff might have aided the great basketball teams of the year: De Paul, Indiana, Kentucky, and even Ohio State. Instead, Digger felt that many of the great college basketball seniors like Kyle Macy of Kentucky and Mike Woodson and Butch Carter of Indiana should not be watching the game on television, just as he was that evening; that they should have been at Market Square Arena in Indianapolis, suited up and preparing to close their college careers. "The only thing NBC can promote," he said, "is the great freshmen in the country instead of some of the great players and teams that get upset along the way. Until the media start looking into the degrees and majors of many of the college basketball players, we'll be left with people admiring teams that are outstanding on the court and mediocre as people. College basketball fans are buying points and wins; they're not concerned with the athlete's major or personality."

There were also many discouraging stories a coach picked up around the country during the course of a season or a recruiting swing. Among other things, Digger had heard first hand that one successful tournament team had paid $15,000 for one of its players. "I was playing in a celebrity golf tournament," he said, "and the person next to me on the bus trip to the course told me that a group of boosters were raising money so that the head coach could sign a blue-chip recruit. Thirty affluent boosters were kicking in five

hundred dollars apiece to help the coach out." That kind of
violation, laundered through indirect parties, was impossible for the
NCAA to substantiate, and was not uncommon in recruiting battles.
"People will never hear about it," said Digger. "For all they know that
coach could be on television tonight because people focus on
things like the transition game or slam dunks—not the ethics of a
program."

        As the Louisville-UCLA contest progressed it was obvious it
would not be one of the great tournament match-ups, and when
Louisville began to give up a few quick baskets Digger couldn't keep
himself from muttering instructions to Denny Crum: "Just play them
half court man-to-man; throw a zone at them and you beat them. You
can't let UCLA develop a running game—all they do is take their
press offense to score. It's not their regular set offense that hurts
you."

        Presently he drifted back to his college-game observations,
explaining how many college coaches become caught up in the
winning-at-any-expense theory: "Most of these coaches are good
guys; they're just caught up in winning and don't even realize
they're doing it." Whether it be alumni that run the school, the fat
cats or investors who aid a program financially, Digger went on,
there are many different types of pressures some college coaches
feel to win. "A lot of the time it might be that a university president is
worried about being fired by a board of trustees that have athletic
interests," he said. "If there are people on the board like that, or
outsiders who contribute heavily to a school, sometimes a college
yields to a personality who wants that athletic success, because
financially the school just can't afford to break off such an association. They say, 'It's only the Athletic Department, not the English or
Chemistry Department.' That could never happen here at Notre
Dame because the Holy Cross priests run the university and they
don't get involved in that kind of thing. Father Hesburgh and Father
Joyce wouldn't have any part of it. There aren't any sugar daddies
involved with our sports programs and we stay away from alumni or
businessmen helping our athletes in any financial situations."

        Touching on his own sometimes callous manner, he said he
had developed it as a means of self-preservation throughout his
college coaching experience. He also looked to the weeks ahead,
when he could reflect on the season, the coaches' decisions, and

countless other elements that comprise a college basketball program. While Louisville was in the process of beating the Bruins behind Darrell Griffith, Digger sized up his program for the years ahead. "It's going to be tough for us to win it all," he said. "We're going to have to have it all together to beat the type of competition that's spread across the country."

21

A FITTING FINISH

Slater, Missouri, wasn't the end of the world, but it would be the end of Digger's basketball responsibilities until the next fall. The season was now a memory as Digger headed for Joe Kleine's home town. Kleine had signed an institutional letter to attend Notre Dame six months earlier, followed by a national letter of intent in the spring. Digger could not be present when Joe announced his decision because that would have given him too many visits with the family under NCAA guidelines. The recruiting effort had begun in Kansas City on July 25, 1979, as Joe prepared for the AAU games. A year later it would end with a social visit to Slater for a round of golf, a town-wide basketball clinic presentation, and a dinner at the American Legion hall with the Kleine family and some of Slater's better known residents.

There's only one efficient way to get from South Bend to Slater: take Pete Pilliod's private prop jet to the Marshall, Missouri, airport and then rely on someone to drive you from the field to nearby Slater. Pilliod jumped at the chance to make another visit to Slater—despite the threat of being fed hog fries at the Legion hall. Pete had accompanied Digger to Slater twice before, and had taken to the down-home atmosphere of the small town. His last brush with Notre Dame athletics had been the De Paul game which he termed a greater sporting event than a Super Bowl or a championship prizefight. The hysteria that followed the Irish upset of the Blue Demons captivated the furniture manufacturer to a point where he sat for a half hour after the game and watched the reaction. "It was like the last few minutes of an exciting game, only the De Paul game started from that point and built to where you couldn't wait for it to end because you were drained from all the emotion," he recalled. "Then, when it ended, I couldn't believe the celebration." This time, he would find the day in Slater even more relaxing.

John Merk and Jim Thomas, the Slater High School basketball coaches, greeted the plane just before noon. The most challenging task that faced the visitors would be to find the right size of straw cowboy hat and matching feather band at a shop in Marshall before heading for the municipal golf course. Digger and Pete roamed the town like a pair of tourists, their cowboy hats and designed sunglasses giving them away. The community's people were relaxed and hospitable; they went about their daily routines in the pleasant absence of any big-city tension. It was easy to be yourself in Slater; the atmosphere of the town demanded it.

While Irish assistant coach Tommy McLaughlin opted for jogging, Pete and Digger hooked up in a golf match that wouldn't be settled through the first nine holes. On the second playoff hole it appeared Phelps was in trouble after his approach shot hooked left, winding up downhill of the steeply banked green with an asphalt cart path between Digger and the pin. Without a word Phelps pulled a putter from his bag, dropped his cigar and bounced the ball off the asphalt, catching the top of the bank and rolling the ball within four feet of the pin. Stunned by the miraculous shot, Pilliod missed his putt. There was no blood; it was even after eleven holes. Digger had pulled off another one, this time out of his golf bag.

The boom for Slater's economy continued at Leo Galloway's shoe store, where cowboy boots were priced notoriously cheap. Digger had discovered Galloway's on his first trip to Slater, buying a pair of buggy-whip leather boots that became a topic of conversation in South Bend throughout the winter. By the time the entourage left Galloway's, Digger had ordered a pair of lizard-skin boots, while Tommy McLaughlin had selected a pair for Dottie's son. Digger had worn his boots on the trip and Pete found the chance to surround his feet in the stylish western footwear irresistible. Leo Galloway was used to having people drive for hundreds of miles to take advantage of bargains, but it was rare that people came in by plane for shopping sprees at his place.

The trip to Kleine country wouldn't have been complete without meeting up with Digger's friends, Shorty Haines, the town undertaker, and Frank Markovich, the Slater pharmacist. The pair were true-blue Notre Dame; Frank's son, "Marko," had been Digger's first trainer at Notre Dame. Word of the visit had reached Omaha, where "Marko" was now in pharmacy school. He was also taking time off from his studies to make the four-hour trip to Slater. Mrs.

Markovich was busy preparing a country spread when the travelers arrived at the Legion. The Kleines were all in attendance for the informal banquet, including Joe's grandmother, famous from Slater to South Bend for her homemade apple pie. When her grandson was young, Mrs. Kleine had fed Joe apple pie during Irish basketball broadcasts, advising him that Notre Dame was the place to play his college career. Big Joe, who grew up to resemble former Notre Dame All-America tight end Dave Casper, followed his grandmother's instructions. With guidance and apple pie like that, it had been Notre Dame hands down when Joe chose his college.

As expected, Shorty and Frank came up with a few good stories and a bottle of Bailey's Irish Cream to finish the festivities, while Joe Kleine, Sr. made a few brief after-dinner comments with Digger, Pete, and Frank. Digger advised his hosts "not to be fooled when the grass looks greener outside of the Slater community. What you've got here is something special." Then, with an apple pie tucked under his arm, he prepared for the final stop of the day, the coaching clinic at the high school.

A couple of hundred basketball players, coaches, and parents had gathered in the Slater gymnasium to hear Digger. He had agreed to talk for an hour about college basketball and some technical points of the game, but instead, he used the first twenty minutes to speak of the role of athletics and academics in life, and of how the two elements related to society. He preached the importance of studying hard and striving to be one's own person in whatever career one chose. In particular, he emphasized the point that very few basketball players are good enough to make a living at the sport, pointing to Los Angeles Laker star Magic Johnson as one player in ten thousand. Finally he went into action, calling for two squads of volunteers, whom he used in a demonstration of defensive tactics. He showed each player how to keep his man from a rebound by using a forearm move on the first shot of the game. "How often do you see a referee call more than one foul on that first shot?" he asked. "Set the tone from the first play." The demonstration ended with a lesson in free-throw shooting, after which Digger fielded questions from players and coaches. Then it was back to South Bend.

The Slater trip was the last serious basketball commitment of the year for Digger; it was an experience to reflect on as the 1979–80 Irish basketball season concluded. And, as Digger and his companions recapped the day's events over a few cold beers thousands of feet above the ground, there was also time to think about the next season. It would be another year, a new opportunity to search for the right chemistry to carry the Irish to that elusive national championship. Digger had tried different styles in his nine seasons at Notre Dame and he already knew his strategy for his tenth. He opened a beer and explained that plan:

"The democracy is over."

Appendix

THE SYSTEM

Multiplicity is the key word in the Notre Dame basketball system. It applies to offense, defense, and personnel. Digger Phelps takes the collective talent he's given, blends his men into specific and often different roles, adjusts constantly to other teams on the schedule and—of course—tries to win every game. Naturally, once the playoffs start it's a new season, open for any team to win. Yet during the main season the coaches try constantly to put game plans together—based on knowing which player can do which things at which time. They'll chart possible defenses during the game to select the best two, not just for the second half of a game, but also for the playoffs. To be able to adjust to different offensive attacks is the key to multiple defense.

The same holds true for offense. The team that makes the correct game adjustments wins. In a forty-minute game, Digger looks for that one offensive spurt that will seal the win, no matter when it happens—whether in the first half with twelve minutes left, in the second half with three minutes left, or on a buzzer shot (Tracy Jackson versus Villanova or Maryland).

Digger will tell you that he doesn't think today's game is an easy one to coach successfully because of the widespread super-talent all around the country. To be successful, a team has to have multiple offense and defense. Planned multiple options can neutralize any opposing team's talent.

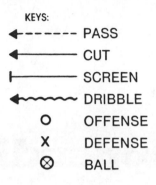

KEYS:

←------- PASS
←——————— CUT
⊢——————— SCREEN
←∿∿∿∿ DRIBBLE
O   OFFENSE
X   DEFENSE
⊗   BALL

OFFENSIVE ALIGNMENTS

The basic man-to-man offensive philosophy is to read the defense and react. The Irish *passing game* offense is relatively simple: (A) If the defense plays the passing lanes—the offense can cut inside for layups and (B) if the defense plays a sagging defense—the offense can move to exterior positions for outside shooting. Patience will bring the shots you want and usually both types occur in most game situations. Offensive rebounding also comes by reading shot angles which give a lot of points.

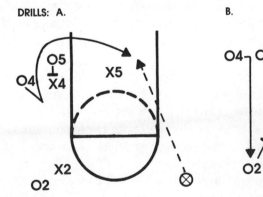

DRILLS: A.

Sag by X4 gets 04 a jumpshot

B.

Playing lane by X4 gives 04 a layup

Digger loves to run the *fast break* which gives any offensive team quick scoring opportunities. The key is the defensive rebound (five people checking their man). He teaches the rebounder to explode out (dribble) to find someone open down court, pass it to him, and beat the other team down the floor before they can set their defense:

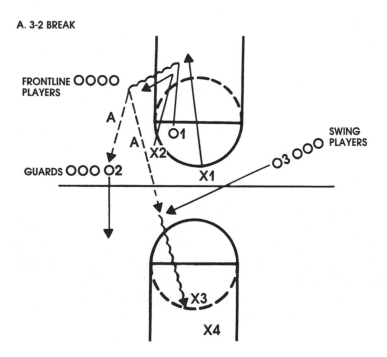

X2 and X1 pressure O1 rebounding of O1's pass off the backboard— then he rebounds and dribbles out looking for O3 and O2. Walk-ons X3 and X4 play defense. All players rebound and explode as well as play with both outlet areas. (Run this drill both sides of floor).

B. 3-2-1 BREAK

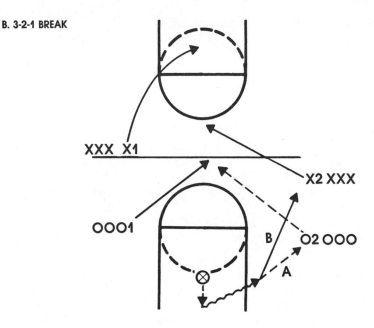

A lot of coaches use this drill: 3 offensive players break down court: Coach yells go to defensive players X1–X2 at ideal time. X2 picks up ball handler and goes to basket. After 3–2 score X1 and X2 bring ball down on O1 for a 2 on 1 fast-break situation. This drill teaches defense and offense.

Against *zones* the Irish tend to play the best shooters in their favorite scoring areas. Versus point defensive zone they'll go 2–1–2.

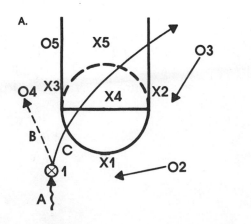

OPTIONS: Cutters can go ballside or opposite.

Against 2 guard, front zone will go 1–3–1

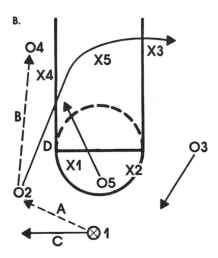

B.

OPTIONS: Cutters can go ballside or opposite. Roll post-HiLo post by holding 04 in post.

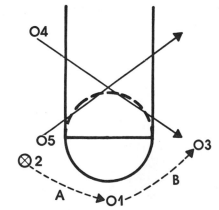

C.

Crisscross 4-5 in post.

Against *presses* Phelps teaches to keep the dribble and use short passes, then explode to basket, e.g., press set vs. zone press:

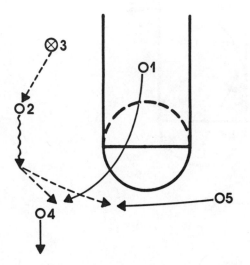

Assume 02 gets open 05 flashes,
01 goes ball sideline 04 goes long,
03 is safety-then dribble by 02 looking for 05 or 01-
then pass looking to explode for a quick score.

Basically Notre Dame's *offensive philosophy* is to *keep it simple* and adjust to the player's talent.

DEFENSES

Along with a basic man-to-man defense Phelps feels that his teams must have multiple defenses. Digger got the *Match-Up Zone* from Bill Green of Marion, Indiana, who had great success in high school with two straight state championships. Bill comes up each fall and puts in his Match-Up Zone during practices and the Irish have had great success with it. The basic concept is as follows:

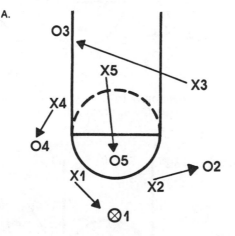

Key always stay with numbers and X1
X1 is the quarterback and picks up who he wants
X2 picks up first man left of X1
X4 picks up first man right of X1
X5 always picks up a post man high or low
X3 picks up open man (rover)

B. On cutters you can follow pass.
C. On cutter you can go opposite pass.

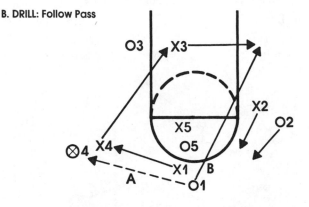

X1 follows pass to O4 - X4 slides to O3.
X3 picks up O1 in corner X2 stays with O2.

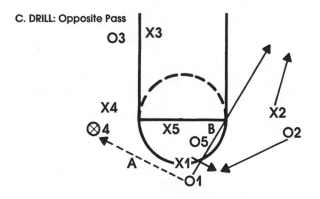

X2 picks up O1's cut to corner.
X1 picks up O2's cut to point.

These are the basic rules of Bill Green's Match-Up Zone. The Irish use it as one of their multiple defenses. Digger will also use a straight 1–3–1 zone or a straight 2–3 zone. At times he will press full court, man-to-man, or zone. The key in a game situation is to find the defense that an opponent can't handle and stay with it.

MAN TO MAN DEFENSIVE CONCEPTS

There are twelve basic offensive concepts that apply to many coaching philosophies against man-to-man defenses. Notre Dame uses the following defensive concepts to handle these situations:

1. GIVE - GO: **B. JAB: GO:**

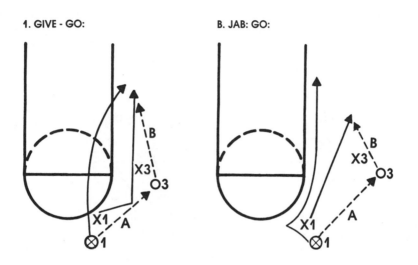

In both situations X1 should take a step to the pass (O3) so that on O1's cut to the basket X1 is always between the ball O3 and his man O1 in order to take away the return passing lane.

2. SHUFFLE CUT: **B. WEAKSIDE:**

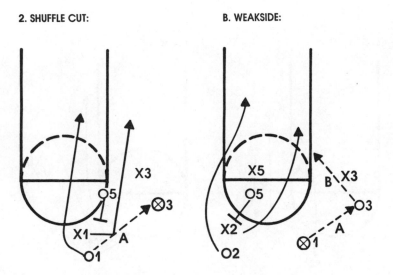

    In both situations X1 and X2 should always *be on the ball side* of the screen in order to be in the passing lane of O1 and O2 cuts. X5 should also talk to X1 and X2 (yell "screen!") and also look to take an offensive charge on O1 and O2 cuts to the basket.

3. DOWNSCREEN

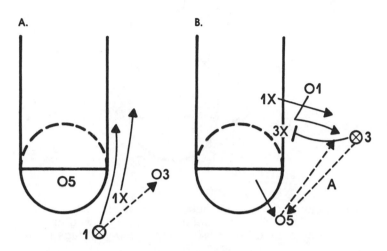

A.

B.

X1 should drop step to the baseline and go around O3's screen. O3 has to remain stationary with the screen or it becomes a moving screen (offensive foul).

4. UPSCREEN:

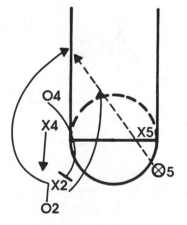

X4 must talk to *X2 who MUST slide ballside of the screen* to take away the passing lane. X4 can delay his recovery to O4 since we are more concerned about O2's layup (high percentage shot). In some situations we can switch if this becomes a problem with a moving screen by the O4 player.

5. EXCHANGE
   (invert)

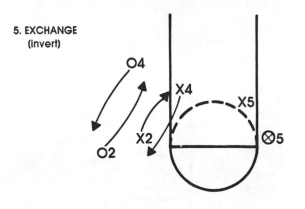

No screening concept but just an exchange in offensive positions. Always allow the defensive player moving to the basket room to slide thru. *(Take away high percentage shot)*.

6. FLASH - POST UP

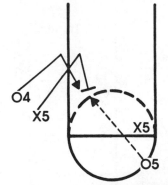

On any flash to the middle or baseline, X4 should drop step to the baseline to force O4 high. Once in the post X4 should get high side between O4 and the passing lane.

7. SPLITS

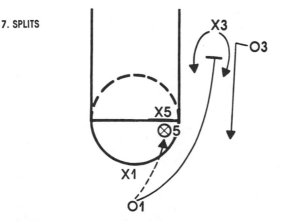

O1 will screen for O3 after a post pass (O5). X1 must talk to X3 about the screen by O1. X3 must read the screen and slide thru or go over the top. X1 can help but MUST recover to O1. Sometimes we can switch or screen split situations.

8. BACKDOOR - ROTATION

A.

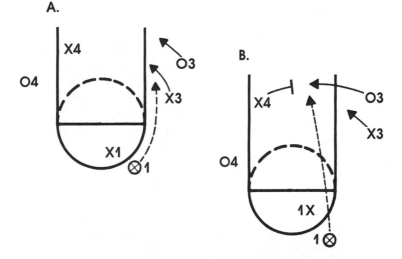

B.

X3 should only allow his arm to be in the passing lane of O1 to O3. Too many times he will overcommit with his body in the passing lane and O3 will "backdoor" (cut to the basket) for an easy pass. If this happens (B) X4 must rotate to help on O3. X3 should still pick up O3 and then X4 would recover to O4.

9. SCREEN TO BALL:

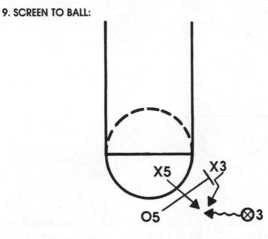

   O5 screens X3. X5 must step out to force O3 wider so that X3 can slide over the top of O5's screen and pick up O3. X5 recovers to O5.

10. SCREEN AWAY FROM BALL:

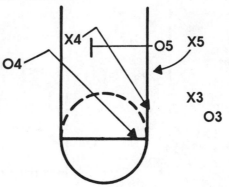

   O5 screens away to X4 for O4. X4 must drop step to baseline and slide thru the screen to recover to O4. X5 helps by giving X4 room to slide thru and then recovers to screener O5.

11. CURL

A.

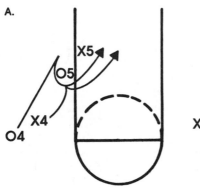

STACK CURL

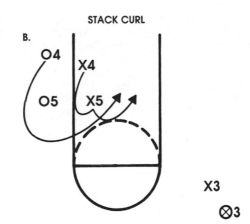

O4 takes his man baseline and curls around O5 screen. X4 must *be ball side of O5* at all times. X5 can help but must recover to O5. We can switch in this situation.

12. DOUBLES:

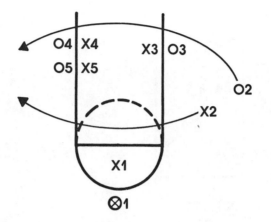

X2 should go top side of 4 screen keep O2 on baseline-stay in passing lane on O1. If problem occurs switch can happen with help from X4 or X5.